W9-CMU-934

Journey to Jericho

by Kaye England

ME Publications
1606 Santa Monica Blvd.
Santa Monica, CA 90404

Acknowledgements:

The long hours necessary to finish this project meant I was absent from my quilt shop more than usual, but the staff of ladies have carried on and quite frankly very well. Most of their work is in the book so not only have they kept the store going, but have been quite involved in the book as well. Thanks to each of you – Alice, Brenda, Caryl, Gachia, Geneva, Joanie, Kathy, Kathleen, Paula, Terri, and yes, even you Gloria. What gems you are. A special thanks to my students, who so generously shared their quilts for the book.

Special thanks go to: Alice Cunningham for her assistance in piecing, binding and quilting; Joanie Rohn for her assistance in piecing; Gloria Barron for her artwork in the quilting designs; Brenda Papadakis for her assistance in manuscript preparation.

©1992. Kaye England. No portion of this book may be reproduced by any means without written permission of the author except for block piece templates, appliqué templates, and quilting design templates. These may be copied for personal use only. The author may be contacted through the publisher.

Graphic design and layout by Shimp Personalized Publication Services, Inc., Las Vegas, NV.

Photography by Michael Negley, Los Angeles, CA.

Printed in the USA.

ISBN: 0-929950-08-9

Table of Contents

Dedication

In loving memory of my father and brother,
Robert Matthews Brown and Robert Rex Brown.

From Jerusalem to Jericho

The inspiration for this quilt is taken from the Scripture relating the parable of the Good Samaritan. (Luke 10:37-37)

And Jesus answering said, "A certain man went down from Jerusalem to Jericho and fell among thieves which stripped him of his raiment, and wounded him, and departed, leaving him half-dead. And by chance there came down a certain priest that way and when he saw him, he passed by on the other side. And likewise, a Levite, when he was at that place, came and looked on him, and passed by on the other side. But a certain Samaritan, as he journeyed, came where he was; and when he saw him, he had compassion on him, and went to him, and bound up his wounds, pouring in oil and wine, and set him on his own beast, and brought him to an inn, and took care of him. And on the morrow when he departed, he took out two pence, and gave them to the host, and said unto him, 'Take care of him; and whatsoever thou spendest more, when I come again, I will repay thee.' Which now of these three, thinkest thou, was neighbor unto him that fell among thieves?" And He said, "He that showed mercy on him." Then said Jesus unto him, "Go, and do thou likewise."

Jerusalem means "possession of peace." Jericho means "a place of fragrance."

In planning this quilt I've tried to incorporate as many of the signs and symbols of Christianity as possible. My hope is that this quilt will be as meaningful to you and your family as it is to me.

Choosing the size of block for this quilt became quite a challenge. Numerous quilts have been done using a twelve inch block. Ten inches seemed to be the next choice, but there were a number of publications using some of the blocks in that size. Obviously, these blocks have all been taken from old files so the size needed to be different in order to create a fresh look. Therefore, after much thought, I decided upon an eight inch block. Eight is the number of the Resurrection, for it was on the eighth day after His entry into Jerusalem that Christ rose from the grave.

Twelve, the number of pieced blocks in the quilt, has always been a favorite number in Christian symbolism. It is the number of Apostles and is occasionally used to represent the entire Church.

There are six alternate blocks, six being the number of creation and perfection. These symbolize divine power, majesty, wisdom, love, mercy, and justice.

There are ten side blocks, the number of the Ten Commandments. The four corner blocks represent the four evangelists, Matthew, Mark, Luke, and John.

Three was called by Pythagorus the number of completion, expressive of a beginning, a middle, and an end. In Christian symbolism, three became the divine number suggesting the Trinity and also the three days that Christ spent in the tomb. This number could then be symbolic of the completed quilt: the top, a beginning, batting, the middle, the backing, an end!

The bible has greatly influenced quiltmakers for many years and as a quiltmaker I became thoroughly consumed by the stories surrounding the chosen names for each block. I also have somewhat of a heritage in quilting as my paternal grandmother, Delilah Allien Matthews Brown, was a quilter – leaving a legacy of some wonderful quilts, one of which resides very happily with me. There is a wealth of research material available and I became a sponge. I chose twelve blocks from among many, mostly because I liked the design or that the stories were so rich with meaning!

The beginning of this story was a yearning to teach a class on the bible blocks and their meanings. After many months of study and teaching, it became apparent that there was a wonderful story emerging and so with the help of many friends we began. The title was chosen as a good friend and I were scanning loads of material and there it was: The parable of the Good Samaritan has a passage that reads, "From Jerusalem to Jericho," and in that instant a name was chosen. Words could never explain how very important my friends and family have been to me during this project. How could one ever undertake such a task without the love and support of others! My life has been full and happy, but as this nears completion I find a new feeling emerging and believe it is somewhat relief that the end is near but mostly I feel it's a culmination of the warm feelings generated by all my support group.

I owe so many so much that I fear I'll overlook some names so just know that I'm ever grateful to each of you. I must give a personal thanks to Mary Ellen Hopkins, my good friend, whose teachings and encouragement to grow have been invaluable. My first teaching seminar was with Mary Ellen and it has been a catalyst for my quilting life. Hopefully her zest and approach to quilting will be contagious. Thanks as well to David Hopkins, for his constant words of support and encouragement. Special thanks to John and Mimi Shimp for their patience and ability to take my unorganized thoughts and create a book.

As the book was nearing completion, my mother became very ill and has spent some time with me recuperating. She has sat and watched as the computer clicked away and slowly renewed herself. I've so enjoyed having her with me and I think she has enjoyed watching the book close. Even though my dedication was to my father and brother, Mother, please know you mean the world to me and without your care and support all these years I would not be where I am.

My wonderful husband David has always been there for me and forever been my support. I thank you so much. My children and their spouses, Bryan and Julie England, and Sheila and Kenneth Richards, have patiently waited for their quilts to be finished. It seems I am constantly putting other projects ahead of their quilts! I want them to know they are a constant source of pride for me and I love them dearly. I am especially thankful for my wonderful granddaughters Chelsea Kaye and Morgan Taylor Richards. Your Nana wishes you a life rich with happiness. I believe grandchildren are our assurance that the prized quilts we produce will have a loving home awaiting them.

As you begin your journey from Jerusalem to Jericho, may it be a fulfilling and enjoyable trip. I have so enjoyed the road.

Lord, my heart is not haughty, nor mine eyes lofty: neither do I exercise myself in great matters, or in things too high for me. (Ps 131:1)

The Blocks
and
Their Stories

This is the layout I chose for the blocks in this quilt. Smaller quilts can be made with fewer blocks, and the layouts may vary. There are a multitude of possible quilts to be made from these blocks. See the section starting on page 93 for examples.

David and Goliath

David (beloved), the eighth and youngest son of Jesse, a citizen of Bethlehem. Jesse appears to have been a humble man. His mother's name is not recorded. Some think she was the Nahash of II Samuel 17-25. As to his personal appearance, we know that he was "red haired, with beautiful eyes and goodly to look at." (I Sam 16-12:17:42.)

Goliath (great), a famous giant of Gath, who for forty days openly defied the armies of Israel, but was at length slain by the younger and weaker David. He was probably a descendant from the Rephaim, who found refuge among the Philistines after they were dispersed by the Ammonites. (Deut 2:20:21) Goliath's sword was preserved at Nob as a religious trophy. (I Sam 21:9)

David's victory over Goliath was a turning point in his life and he rose to prominence through the extraordinary courage he displayed tackling the huge Philistine, Goliath. The bravery of this shepherd boy, who armed with a simple slingshot, defeated this heavily armed giant, is still proverbial. Their battle took place during renewed fighting with the Philistines after Saul's victory in Michmash. Up to that point, the account of Saul's kinship in I Samuel largely focuses on Saul's acts of disobedience. The real hero David emerges.

It appears that an impasse had been reached between the Philistine and Israelite armies. They faced each other from adjacent hillsides across a valley. Then the Philistine champion Goliath, of enormous size (the Bible accounts "six cubits and one span" is equivalent to more than nine feet, or three meters, covered with heavy armor), issued a challenge of a one on one combat. No one accepted until David heard that Saul might offer his lovely daughter to whomever would challenge and slay Goliath.

David volunteered to be Israel's champion after seeing that the armies of the living God were being shamed by a heathen giant. David, refusing any armor for protection because he found it uncomfortable, picked up some stones from the river bed and armed only with his sling and shepherd's staff, walked toward the giant.

Goliath was insulted that a person of such boyish appearance and apparently such simple weapons should dare approach him spoke to David saying, "Am I a carrion dog, that thou comest out against me with nought but a staff in thy hand? Come to me, and I will give thy flesh unto the fowls of the air, and to the beasts of the fields." (I Sam 17:43-44)

David, ever cautious watching the Philistines, stepped alertly and paced well beyond javelin cast, circling about Goliath so that he could bring the giant face-to-face with him against the blazing sun. And as he was doing so, he called across the stillness to Goliath. "Thou hast come out against me, armed with sword and spear and javelin. A brazen shield is on thine arm and thou art hung heads to foot with armor of brass. But if this be all they strength, beware of it! For I am come out against thee in the name of the Lord of Hosts, the God of the armies of Israel, whom thou hast insulted and defied, and this day the Lord will deliver thee into my hand. And I will smite thee. That all the earth may know there is a God in Israel, and that His salvation is not in sword and spear, nor His battle to the strong, but that He giveth victory according as His decree." Then, before Goliath could strike a single blow, David ran towards the giant with the speed of an angel sent from God, whirling his sling above his head, his gaze fixed gravely on his huge target. Then David lifted his thumb and set the stone sailing through the air and smote the Philistine in the middle of his forehead, and without a groan, the giant fell face down upon the ground. (I Sam 17:49) Seeing their champion slain, the Philistines fled. This one act endeared David to Saul and started David's rise to power.

Block Construction

There are six main pieces for this block. Note the placement of the pieces and select fabric colors

and values for each piece to provide your intended meaning in the block. Use the provided templates as necessary to cut the pieces shown here and construct them as shown below.

- Make two "A" sections using number 4, 5, and 6 pieces. Sew the pairs of number 6's together, then sew these together with the number 5. Finally, add number 4.

- Make one "B" section by sewing together three number 5 pieces.

- Make four "C" sections using number 1, 2, and 3. Sew the 2's with the 3's and combine these pairs. As you combine these two pairs, stitch to within one seam allowance of the point where the number 1 piece is to be added. Then set in the number 1 piece.

- The "D" sections are number 4 pieces.

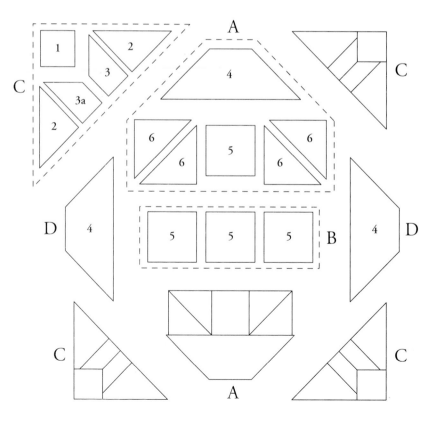

10

- Sew the two "A" sections to the "B" section.

- Sew the two "D" sections to opposite sides.

- Sew the four "C" sections to the corners.

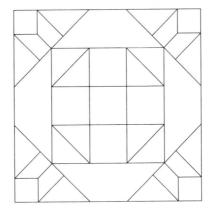

Finished Block

Templates

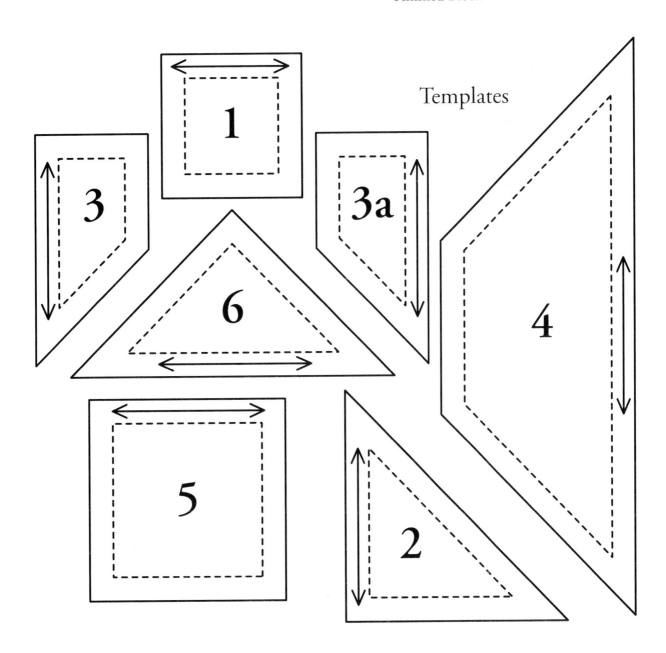

King David's Crown

"So all the elders of Israel came to the king to Hebron; and King David made a league with them in Hebron before the Lord: and they anointed David king over Israel." (II Sam 5:3)

In the days following the death of Samson, while the Israelites were still embattled against the Philistines, Samuel, the son of Hannah, came to be recognized as a true prophet of the Lord. The people of Israel appealed to Samuel that he anoint one of their own people to be king. The first to be chosen by Samuel was the great warrior Saul. He fought mightily against the enemies of Israel, but because of his idolatries, the Lord turned against him and rejected him as king of the Israelites. It was then that the Lord directed Samuel as to how he could find David, son of Jesse, and appoint him as Israel's King.

After rejecting Saul as king of Israel, the Lord instructed the prophet Samuel to fill his horn with oil and go. "I will send thee to Jesse the Bethlehemite; for I have provided me a king among his sons." (I Sam 16:1)

As a consequence of his heroic deeds David's popularity awakened a jealousy in Saul (I Sam 18:6-16), which showed itself in different ways. Saul developed a bitter hatred toward David and planned his death in various ways. (I Sam 17:30) All the plans of the jealous king failed and in fact only endeared this young hero more to the people and most distressing to Saul, his own son Jonathan developed a life-long bond of friendship with David. After one attempt at reconciliation had failed, David eventually found protection with Israel's arch-enemy, Achish, King of Philistine Gath.

David was given the town of Kiklag as his home and there he lived for sixteen months, forming his own army from Israelites that were opposed to Saul. This army lived by thievery from the tribes of He Negreb. This proved to be a great mistake as they took their revenge on David when he had marched north to fight Saul at Gilboa. Upon his return, he found that his town had been destroyed and his two wives abducted. He pursued them and after catching them by surprise, he massacred them and recovered his wives. David was then told of Saul's death. (II Sam 1) An Amalekite brought Saul's crown and bracelet and laid them at his feet. David and his men mourned for Saul. David composed a beautiful ode – a "lamentation over Saul and over Jonathan his Son." (II Sam 1:18-27) Entitled "The Bow", it was to be taught to all children in Jonathan and Saul's memory.

Soon after David became king, he was forced to again fight the Philistines, whom he defeated in two great battles. He chose his followers and went to Judah to recapture the Ark of God, which had fallen in the hands of the Philistines. He triumphantly returned to Jerusalem with the Ark, which he then made both the political and religious capital of the State. (II Sam 6) David's entrance into Jerusalem has been interpreted as foretelling Christ's entry into the city prior to the Passion.

In describing the passage of the Ark of God into Jerusalem, it is recounted that "David went and brought the Ark of God from the house of Obed-edom into the city. "David then placed the Ark in a tabernacle which he had built for this purpose. Having the Ark in Jerusalem meant that God Himself was now here consecrating it as a Holy City.

Having reached the height of his glory, David ruled over a great empire and he was rich beyond compare. But in the midst of all this success he fell and his character became stained with the sin of adultery. (II Sam 11:2-27) His obsession of Bathsheba caused him to wrong Uriah, an officer of the Gibborim, the corps of heroes. (II Sam 23:29) By his orders Uriah was "set in the front of the hottest battle" in order to cause his death. Nathan the prophet was sent by God to bring home his crimes. David bitterly bewailed his sins before God. The thirty-second and fifty-first Psalms unveil the battle of his soul and eventually his spiritual recovery. Bathsheba finally became his wife after Uriah's death. In punishment for having caused his death the Lord caused the death of David and Bathsheba's first-born. After the child's death, David was forgiven. He then repented and a second child was born to David and Bathsheba. The child was named Solomon. (II Sam 12: 24-25)

More cloudy and dark days fell upon David. His oldest son Amnon, whose mother was Ahinoam of Jezreel, was charged with a great and shameful crime. (II Sam 13:14) This seemed to be the beginning of the disasters in his later years. Absalom avenged the crime against his sister Tamar and put Amnon to death. This greatly troubled David's heart as his love for Absalom allowed him to forget his duty as King and he permitted Absalom to flee into Geshur beyond Jordan.

A great famine of three years fell upon the land. (II Sam 21:1-14) Only to be followed by a pestilence brought upon the land as more punishment for David's sinful pride in numbering the people. In a span of three days more than 70,000 people perished. (II Sam 24:2) Absalom, extremely bitter over his forced exile, rebelled against David. He gradually gained over the people and was proclaimed King in Hebron. David, now fearing his life, left Jerusalem. (II Sam 15:13-20) Absalom later met his fate by the hand of Joab in war. (II Sam 18:9-18) The death of his rebellious son filled David's heart with the most poignant grief. He went up to the chamber over the gate, and wept; and as he went, thus he said, "O my son Absalom, my son, my son Absalom! Would God I had died for thee, O Absalom, my son, my son!" (II Sam 18:33) Peace was finally restored and David returned to Jerusalem and resumed his reign.

After the suppression of the rebellion of Absalom, David lived ten peaceful years. His exciting and laborious life and all the dangers and trials through which he had passed had left him an aged man, old beyond his years. He became aware that his life was nearing an end. This caused a conspiracy to break out in the palace as to whom would be his successor. Nathan hastened on a decision on the part of David in favor of Solomon. Solomon was brought to Jerusalem, and anointed king and seated on his father's throne. (I Kings 1:11-53) David's last words revealed his unwavering faith in God and his joyous confidence in His gracious covenant promises. (II Sam 23:1-7)

Having reigned forty years and six months (II Sam 5:5; I Chr 3:4), David died (BC 1015) at the age of seventy years, and was buried in the city of David. His tomb is on Mount Zion.

The Psalms of David is a common title for the Book of Psalms. David was the largest contributor to the collection. About eight psalms are attributed to David.

As is the case of most great people, David's greatness was not felt until he was gone. He had lived in harmony with both the priesthood and the prophets; a sure sign that the spirit of his government had been thoroughly loyal to the higher aims of the theocracy. His nation had not been able to oppress him, but had been left in the free enjoyment of its ancient liberties. David's weak indulgence to his sons as well as his own sins had been atoned and were forgotten at his death in the remembrance of his lifelong deeds. He reigned thirty-three years in Jerusalem and seven and a half at Hebron. (II Sam 5:5) A great legacy was passed on to his son Solomon.

Block Construction

There are five main pieces for this block. Note the placement of the pieces and select fabric colors and values for each piece to provide your intended meaning in the block. Use the provided templates as necessary to cut the pieces shown here and construct them as shown below.

- Make two "A" sections for the top and bottom row of the block, using number 1, 2, and 3 pieces.

  Sew four number 3's together.

  Sew pairs of number 1 triangles together. Make two of these for each side.

  Combine these in a row as shown, with a number 2 square at each end.

- Make two "B" sections by doing the above without the number 2 squares at the end.

- Make the center "C" section using number 5 pieces, the number 4 square, and number 1 triangles.

  Sew a number 5 piece onto each side of the square.

  Sew the number 1 triangles onto the corners.

- Sew the "B" sections to opposite sides of the "C" section.

- Sew the "A" sections to the other two sides.

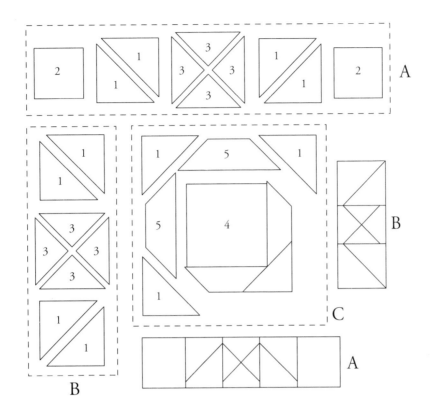

A

B

B

C

A

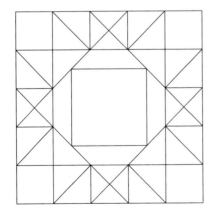

Finished Block

Templates

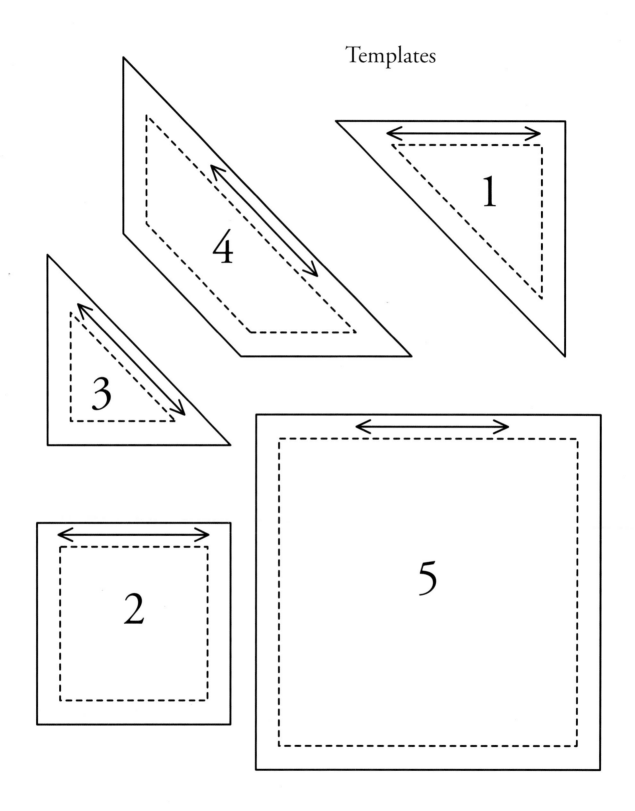

Jacob's Ladder

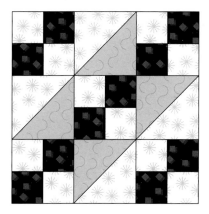

"And he lighted upon a certain place, and tarried there all night, because the sun was set; and he took of the stones of that place and put them for his pillows and lay down in that place to sleep. And he dreamed, and behold a ladder set upon the earth, and the top of it reached to heaven; and behold the angels of God ascending and descending on it." Gen 28:11-12

Jacob – one who follows on another's heels: supplanter. (Gen 25:26; 27:36)

According to Genesis 25:23, the rivalry between Jacob and Esau, Isaac's twin sons, was foretold before they were born. During her difficult pregnancy, Rebekah went to a holy place to consult with God and was told: There are two nations in your womb, your issue will be two rival peoples. One nation will have the mastery of the other and the elder will serve the younger."

Esau emerged first and was "red, altogether like a hairy cloak." (Gen 25:25) Then came Jacob, holding on to his brother's heel. Growing up they took separate walks in life. Esau spent his time becoming a skilled hunter which Isaac preferred because he had

a taste for wild game and Jacob preferred a quieter life at home which endeared him to Rebekah (25:28). After returning from a full day of hunting, Esau asked Jacob for some stew and Jacob quickly seized the opportunity to benefit himself from the situation and demanded Esau give up his birthright in return for food. At the time, Esau's hunger overcame his good sense, and he gave his promise to him that his birthright would belong to Jacob. (Gen 25:33)

Years later, when Isaac was old, blind and nearing the end of his life, he wished to give Esau his blessing. Isaac told Esau to hunt game and make a dish he could eat before giving his blessing. Rebekah however, overhearing Isaac, was determined that it would be her favorite Jacob to receive the paternal blessing, so she had Jacob bring two goats to prepare a stew. She then continued her deceit by dressing Jacob in Esau's clothes, placing the goatskins on his arms to imitate Esau's hairy skin and sent him forth to Isaac. Being sightless and aged, Isaac was tricked into believing this was his favored Esau and consequently blessed Jacob in his brother's stead.

Esau returned from his hunting and brought the food he had prepared for his father. Realizing he had been tricked, Isaac trembled with rage, but the blessing given to Jacob was irrevocable. Esau was distraught and cried out, "Now he has supplanted me twice. First he took my birthright and now he has taken my blessing." (Gen 27:36) He then planned that after Isaac's death he would kill Jacob in revenge. Rebekah, fearing for Jacob's life, sent him to her brother Laban, in Haran, far to the North. Jacob was safe there but paid for his deceit by being forced into exile.

Often represented in paintings of the Renaissance is the dream that came to Jacob on his journey to Haran in search of a wife. Stopping at night along the roadside, he took stones for his pillow and lay down to sleep. "And he dreamed, and behold, the angels of God ascending and descending on it." (Gen 28:12) Then the Lord addressed Jacob saying "I am the Lord of Abraham, thy Father, and the God of Isaac. The land whereon thou liest, to thee I will give it, and to thy seed." When Jacob awoke, he realized that the Lord had been with him, and he took the stone of his pillow and constructed a pillar and, pouring oil upon it, called the place Bethel. Moreover, he made a vow that, if God remained with him, "this stone, which I have set for a pillar, and shall be God's house; and of all that thou shalt give me I will surely give the tenth unto thee." (Gen 28:22)

Like other sacred sites associated with the patriarchs, Bethel was originally a sanctuary for Canaanites. The Bible refers to such open-air sanctuaries as bamot, usually translated as "high places". They were often in the shade, "under any spreading tree". (Deut 12:2) Characteristic of these sanctuaries were matsevot or "standing stones". As cult objects, these stones commemorated a divine manifestation, as at Bethel, and were generally regarded as symbols of the divinity. They could also be memorials to the dead. One of the most impressive of the "high places" is at Gezer. Here a row of ten massive stones, dating

from the mid-second millennium BC, bears witness to this ancient form of worship.

While in Haran, Jacob met with Rachel. Laban would not consent to give his daughter in marriage until Jacob had served him for seven years; but to Jacob these years were passed, Laban deceived Jacob, and instead of his beloved Rachel, he gave Leah to Jacob. He then had to serve another seven years before he could take Rachel as his wife. Lifelong sorrow, disgrace, and trials in the retributive providence of God, followed as a consequence of this double union.

After the fourteen years of service, Jacob had a great desire to return to his parents, but at the entreaty of Laban, he spent another six years with him, tending his flocks. (Gen 31) Laban became angry upon learning Jacob had set out on his journey home and overtook him in seven days. The meeting was a painful sort. After much recrimination and reproach directed against Jacob, Laban is finally pacified, and taking an affectionate farewell of his daughters, returns to his home in Padanaram. And now all connection of the Israelites is at an end.

After parting with Laban, Jacob is met by a company of angels, as if to greet him on his return and welcome him back to the Land of Promise. (Gen 32:1, 2) He called the name of the place Mahanaim: i.e. "the double camp", probably his own camp that he had formerly seen, when, twenty years before, the weary solitary traveler, saw the angels of God ascending and descending on the ladder whose top reached to heaven. (Gen 28:12)

Jacob learns with dismay of the approach of his brother with a band of 400 men to meet him. In great agony of mind, he prepares for the worst of meetings. He feels that he must now depend only on God and betakes himself to him in earnest prayer, and sends on before him a present to Esau "a present to my lord Esau from thy servant Jacob." Jacob's family was then transported across the Jabbok; but he himself remained behind, spending the night in communion with God. While thus engaged, there appeared one in the form of a man who wrestled with him. In this mysterious contest, Jacob prevailed, and as a memorial of it, his name was changed to Israel (wrestler with God); and the place where this occurred, he called Peniel, for he said, "I have seen God face-to-face, and my life is preserved." (Gen 32:25-31)

After this anxious night, Jacob went on his way, halting, mysteriously weakened by the conflict, but strong in the assurance of the divine factor. Esau came forth and met him, but his spirit of revenge was appeased, and the brothers met as friends and during the remainder of their lives they maintained family relations. After a brief sojourn at Succoth, Jacob moved forward and pitched his tent near Shechem, but at length, and under Divine Directions, he moved to Bethel, where he made an altar unto God, (Gen 35:6,7) and where God appeared to him and renewed the Abrahamic covenant.

While journeying from Bethel to Ephrath (the Canaan name for Bethlehem), Rachel died while giving birth to her second son, Benjamin, (Gen 35:16-20) fifteen or sixteen years after the birth of Joseph. Jacob then reached the family residence at Mamre to wait by the dying bed of his father Isaac. The complete reconciliation between Esau and Jacob was shown by their uniting in the burial of the patriarch. (Gen 35:27-29)

At length, the end of Jacob's life draws close, and he summons his sons to his bedside that he may bless them. Among his last words, he repeats the story of Rachel's death, although more than forty years had passed since that event took place, but he remembered it as tenderly as if it had happened only yesterday; and when "he had made an end of charging his sons, he gathered up his feet into the bed, and yielded up the Ghost." (Gen 49:33) Jacob's body was embalmed and carried with great pomp into Canaan, and buried beside his wife Leah in the cave of Machpelah, according to his dying charge. There probably, his embalmed body remains to this day. (Gen 50:1-13)

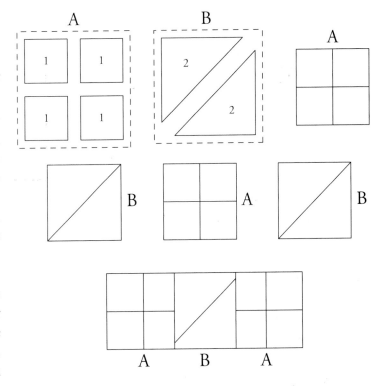

19

Block Construction

There are only two pieces to this block. These are a finished 2⅔" triangle, and a finished a 1⅓" square. Note the placement of the pieces and select fabric to cut for each triangle and square. Consult the section on color meanings as desired in your selections. Use the provided templates as necessary in cutting the pieces. Build your block using the approach shown here, or your own approach.

- Make five "A" sections, each from four number 1 pieces (fabrics in each section may differ.)

- Make two "B" sections, each from two number 2 pieces (fabrics in each section may differ.)

- Combine the sections as indicated in the figure (two rows of "A–B–A" and one row of "B–A–B" in the center.)

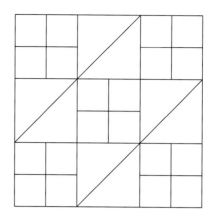

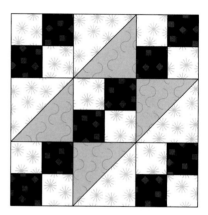

Finished Block

Templates

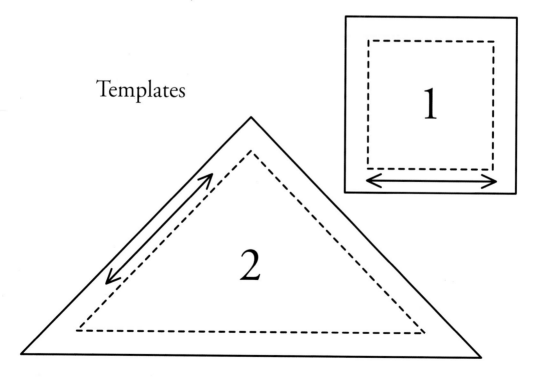

Crown of Thorns

"And the soldiers clothed Him with purple and plaited a crown of thorns and put it about His head and began to salute Him, Hail King of the Jews." (Mark 15:16-18)

The Crown of Thorns is perhaps the most widely known symbol of our Lord's passion. It recalls the hymn lines from Bernard of Clairvaux's Salve caput cruentatum: "O Sacred Head, now wounded with grief and shame weighted down, now scornfully surrounded with thorns, your only crown." Few of our patchwork patterns are as unmistakenly like their name as Crown of Thorns. The spiked wreath of triangles is not an abstraction. We immediately see the intention and most certainly understand.

The Crown of thorns that the soldiers plaited and then forcefully thrust on Christ's head was all a part of the mockery they devised. Before Pontius Pilate, Jesus had borne witness to His Divine Kingship. The soldiers then picked up on this affirmation

in order to ridicule it. They put a robe on Jesus, a crown of thorns on His head and a reed as a make-believe scepter in His right hand. They then beat the crown of thorns into His head inflicting pain of body, but most importantly pain of soul and mind.

It is supposed by some that the Crown of Thorns placed in wanton cruelty by the Roman soldiers on our Saviour's brow before His crucifixion was made of branches of the Zizyphus spina Christi, or Jujube tree. This tree overruns a great part of the Jordan Valley and is referred to as the lotus-tree. The thorns are long, sharp, and curved and often create a festering wound. Christ is usually pictured wearing the Crown of Thorns from this moment until He is taken down from the Cross.

"By the cross, the nail, the thorn, piercing spear, and torturing scorn: that Christ redeemed us. Our debt before God is cancelled, for God set it aside, "nailing it to the cross." (Col 2:14)

Thorns and thorn branches signify grief, tribulation and sin. According to St. Thomas Aquinas, thorn bushes suggest the minor sins, and growing briars, or brambles, the greater ones.

The crown of thorns, when shown in connection with saints, is a symbol of their martyrdom. St. Catherine of Siena is often depicted with the stigmata and the crown of thorns which she received from Christ.

Block Construction

There are three main pieces used in this block. The first is the simple square in each corner of the block. The second (A) is the group of eight triangles (all the same size) making up the sides of the block, and finally the center square.

- Piece four "A" units.

- Piece one center unit.

- Add a square (piece number 1) to each narrow end of two of the "A" units.

- Add the other two "A" units to the side of the center unit.

- Sew these three resulting "rows" together.

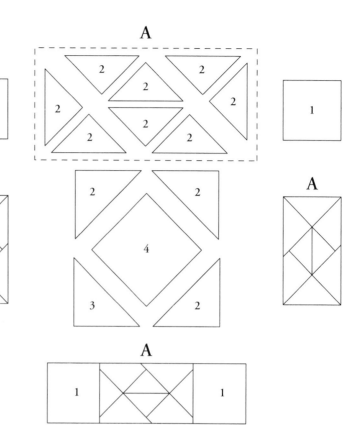

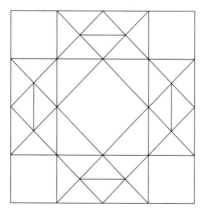

Finished Block

Templates

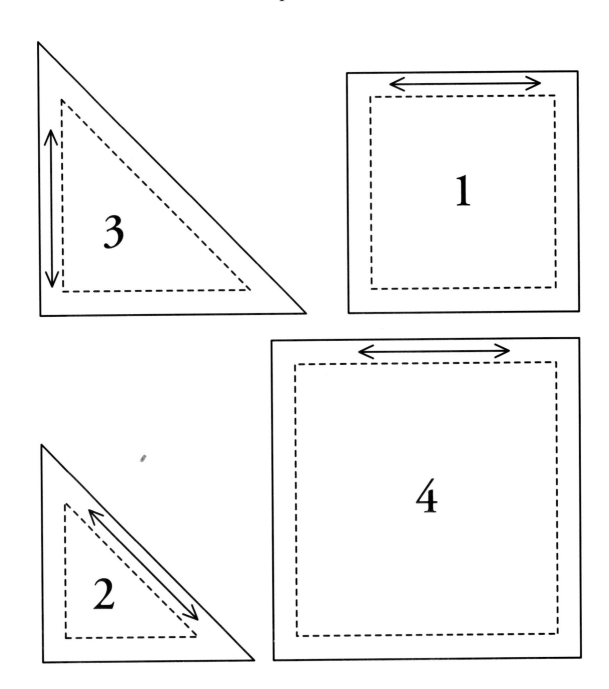

Tree of Life

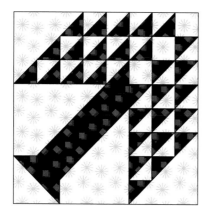

"And the Lord God planted a garden eastward in Eden; and there He put the man whom he had formed. And out of the ground made the Lord God to grow every tree that is pleasant to the sight and good for food; the Tree of Life also in the midst of the garden, and the tree of knowledge of good and evil." (Gen 2:8-10)

Trees have had symbolic significance for all civilizations since the beginning of history. In the Bible, they are a symbol of plenty, goodness, wisdom, and the ideal relationship of work and trust between man and God, in short, the full life. The third chapter of Proverbs explains: "Trust in the Lord with all thine heart; and lean not unto thine own understanding. Happy is the man that findeth wisdom, and the man that getteth her; and happy is everyone that retaineth her. The Lord by wisdom hath founded the earth; by understanding hath he established the heavens."

Philo Judeus, the philosopher of the first century, was first of many theologians to believe that the story of creation was a divine allegory. He believed the Tree of Life was a symbol of religion. Origen, a third

century writer believed that trees were angels, Eden was heaven and all the rivers of the world were wisdom.

According to scripture, the Tree of Life stood in the midst of the Garden of Eden. Writers have had the opinion that this Tree had secret virtues and somehow could preserve life. Most likely the lesson conveyed was that man must seek life not in himself or by his power, but from Him who is Emphatically the Life.

In Proverbs 3:18, wisdom is compared to the Tree of Life: "She is a Tree of Life to them that hold upon her; and happy is everyone that retaineth her." The Tree of Life spoken of in Revelations is an emblem of the joys of the Celestial Paradise. Revelations 2:7 reveals, "He that hath an ear, let him hear what the spirit saith unto the Churches; to him that overcometh will I give to eat of the Tree of Life which is in the midst of the paradise of God." Revelations 22:2 speaks, "In the midst of the street of it, and on either side of the rivers was there the Tree of Life, which bare twelve manner of fruits, and yielded her fruit every month; and the leaves of the Tree were for the healing of the nations." In Revelations 22:14, "Blessed are they that do His commandments, that they may have right to the Tree of Life, and may enter in through the gates into the city."

It is quite obvious that the Tree of Life has played an important part in Christian symbolism. The tree can be a symbol of life, if it is healthy and strong, or a symbol of death if it is poorly nourished and withered.

Genesis 2:9 describes how the Lord planted the Garden of Eden. Genesis then continues relating that the fall of man resulted from Adam accepting the fruit of the Tree of Knowledge. There is a legend that after the death of Adam, the Archangel Michael instructed Eve to plant a branch of the Tree of Knowledge on his grave. From this branch grew the tree which Solomon moved to the Temple garden. It was after discarded and thrown into the pool of Bethesda. There it remained until it was taken out to be made into the Cross.

Block Construction

An easy way to piece this is to break the block down into four sections: the trunk, the crown, and the two sides. Piece each one separately and combine them. The only setting in required is in the trunk section when the two piece 2 triangles are added to the trunk.

- Add pieces 4 and 4a to piece 5, set in the two small triangles (piece 2), and add the larger triangle (piece 6.)

- For the sides and the crown, combine the piece 2 triangles in pairs to make squares.

- For the sides, combine the piece 2 triangle squares into rows and sew the rows together. Then add the piece 1 triangle.

- Make the rows for the crown by sewing the piece 2 triangle squares together with a piece 3 square in the appropriate spot in each row, then combine rows.

- Sew the main pieces together in rows.

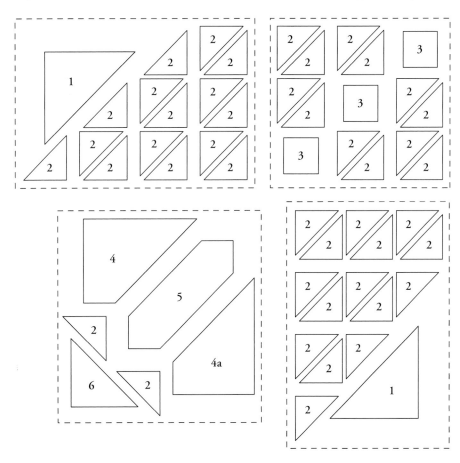

25

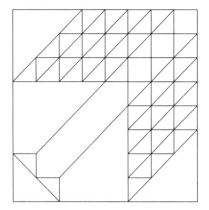 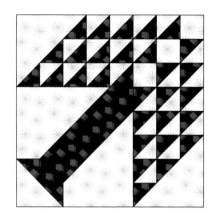

Finished Block

Templates

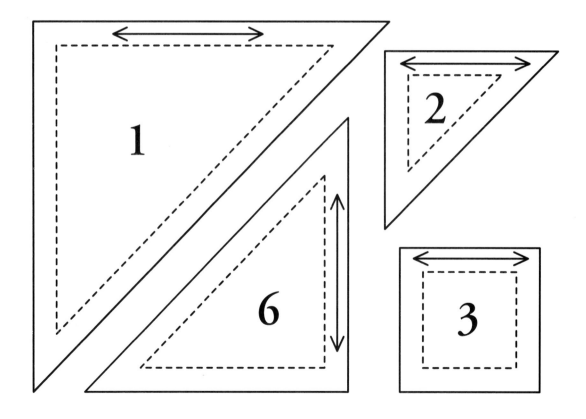

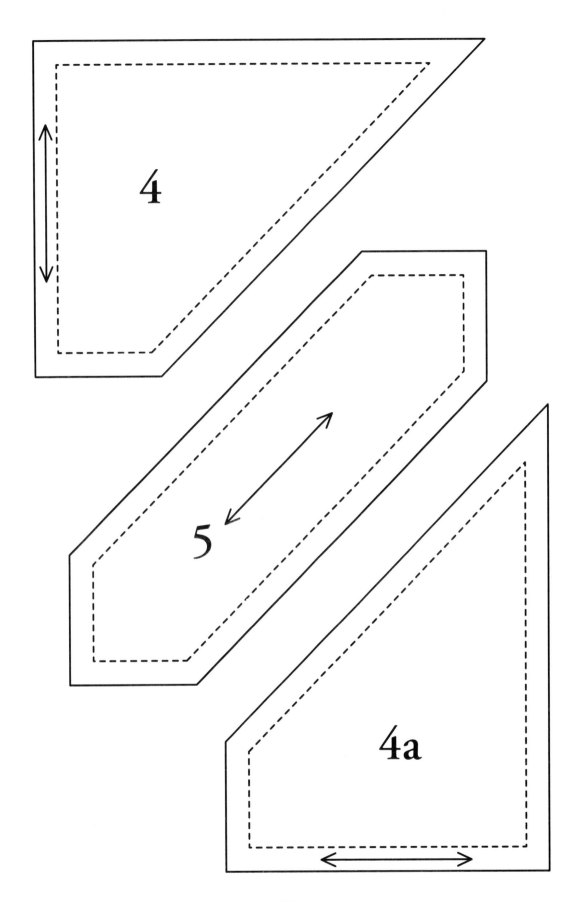

4

5

4a

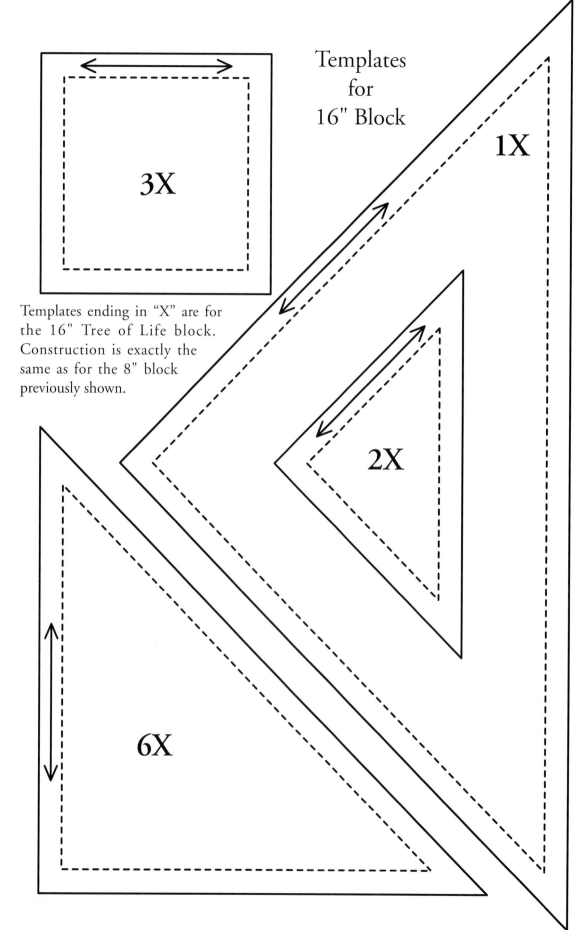

3X

Templates
for
16" Block

1X

Templates ending in "X" are for
the 16" Tree of Life block.
Construction is exactly the
same as for the 8" block
previously shown.

2X

6X

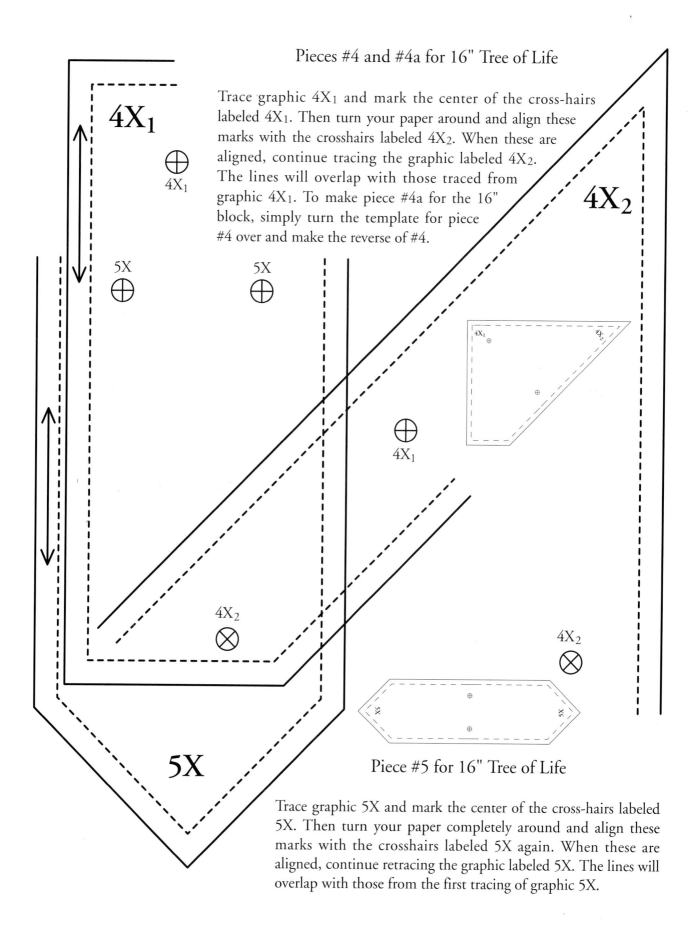

Pieces #4 and #4a for 16" Tree of Life

Trace graphic $4X_1$ and mark the center of the cross-hairs labeled $4X_1$. Then turn your paper around and align these marks with the crosshairs labeled $4X_2$. When these are aligned, continue tracing the graphic labeled $4X_2$. The lines will overlap with those traced from graphic $4X_1$. To make piece #4a for the 16" block, simply turn the template for piece #4 over and make the reverse of #4.

$4X_1$

$4X_2$

5X

5X

$4X_1$

$4X_2$

$4X_2$

5X

Piece #5 for 16" Tree of Life

Trace graphic 5X and mark the center of the cross-hairs labeled 5X. Then turn your paper completely around and align these marks with the crosshairs labeled 5X again. When these are aligned, continue retracing the graphic labeled 5X. The lines will overlap with those from the first tracing of graphic 5X.

Joseph's Coat

"**N**ow Israel loved Joseph more than all his children, because he was the son of is old age: and he made him a coat of many colours." (Gen 37:3)

The elder of two sons of Jacob by Rachel (Gen 30:23-24), who on the occasion of his birth said, "God hath taken away my reproach, the Lord shall add to me another son." Joseph was about six years old when Jacob returned from Haran to Cannan and took up residence in the town of Hebron. "Now Israel loved Joseph more than all his children, because he was the son of his old age,"j41

. and he "made him a long garment with sleeves," i.e., a garment long and full, such as was worn by the children of the nobles. This seems to be the correct rendering of words. The phrase, however, may also be rendered, "A coat of many pieces"– i.e., a patchwork of many small pieces of diverse colors. (Gen 37:35)

When Joseph was about seventeen years old, he incurred the jealous hatred of his brothers. They "hated him and could not speak peaceably unto him. Their anger was increased when he told them of his dreams." (Gens 37:4-5) Finally in a fit of jealous rage, the brothers sold Joseph into slavery to Ishmaelite caravaners travelling to Egypt. Joseph was sold for a mere twenty pieces of silver. The brothers then took Joseph's coat and killed a goat, dipped the coat in the blood and then told their father they had found the blood stained coat in a pit. Joseph, believing a beast had devoured his favoured son, mourned for many days. None of his children were able to console him. "I will go down into the grave unto my son mourning." Thus his father wept for him. (Gen 37:35)

From then onward through a series of adventures, Joseph's fortunes steadily rose. After he was sold to Potiphar an officer of Pharoah's and captain of the guard, he quickly took charge of Potiphar's estates by his honesty and diligence.

Ultimately Joseph's ability to interpret dreams was responsible for his extraordinary career. When Pharoah dreamed of seven fat cows, followed by seven lean cows, Joseph

recognized them. Attempts at punishing them for their evil ways did not last long and Joseph made himself known to them in the land of Goshen. All the brothers came with children and grandchildren led by Jacob. Joseph met his Father and "fell on his neck, and wept on his neck a good while." (Gen 46:29) Jacob said unto Joseph, "Now let me die, since I have seen thy face because thou are yet alive." (Genesis 46:30) Joseph in fulfillment of a promise, went up to Canaan to bury his Father in "the field of Ephron the Hittite." (Gen 49:29-31)

By his wife Asenath, Joseph had two sons, Manasseh and Ephraim. (Gen41:50) Joseph, having obtained a promise from his brethren that when the time should come that God would bring them unto the land which he swore to Abraham, to Isaac, and to

Jacob, they would carry his bones out of Egypt, at length died, at the age of one hundred and ten years, "and they embalmed him, and he was put in a coffin." (Gen 50:26) This promise was faithfully observed. Their descendants, long after, when the Exodus came, carried the body about with them during their forty years of wanderings and at length buried it in Shechem, in the parcel of ground which Jacob bought from the sons of Hamor. (Josh 24:32) With Joseph's death the patriarchal age of the history of Israel came to a close.

Block Construction

The block consists of the center and two each of two side sections. These are constructed separately and then combined.

- Make four each of indicated "A", "B", and "C" sections. Note that the "B" and "C" sections are mirror images of each other.

- Attach a "C" section to the left of each "A" section and a "B" section to the right.

- Attach a number 2 triangle to each side of two of these pieces.

- Make four of the "D" sections and attach a number 5 square to each side of two of these.

- Combine the pieces as shown.

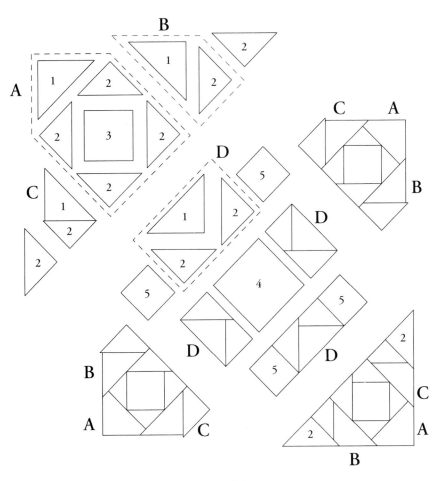

31

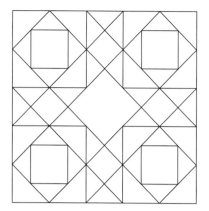 

Finished Block

Templates

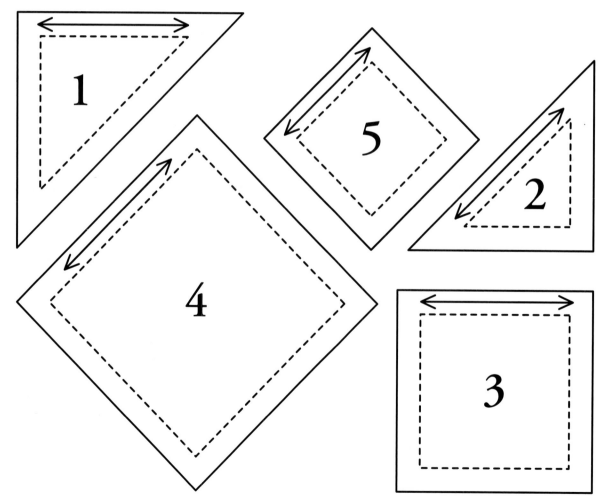

Templates for 16" Block

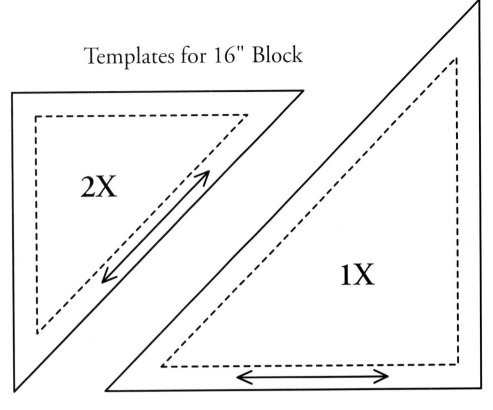

2X

1X

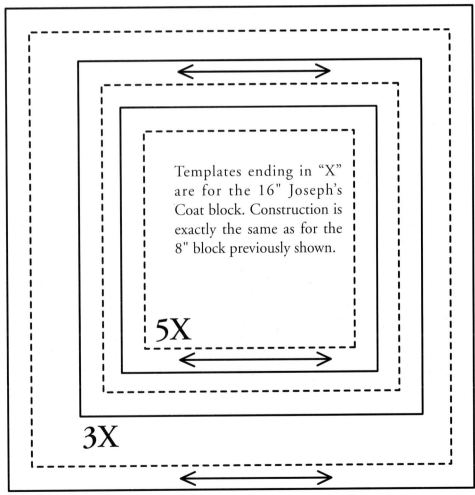

Templates ending in "X" are for the 16" Joseph's Coat block. Construction is exactly the same as for the 8" block previously shown.

5X

3X

4X

Bethlehem Star

"When they had heard the king, they departed; and lo, the star, which they saw in the East, went before them, till it came and stood over where the young child was. When they saw the star, they rejoiced with exceeding great joy." (Matt 2:9-10)

The birth of Jesus was the event that changed the face of the world through Christian religion. According to Matthew, Joseph was going to divorce Mary, to whom he was engaged, because she was pregnant, but was told in a dream that her child had been conceived by the Holy Spirit and should be named Jesus (meaning "Yahweh saves"). So he took her into his home but abstained, and later the child was born.

Next, Matthew relates the story of the Magi. Jesus was born in Bethlehem in the reign of Herod the Great. The Magi, possibly astrologers from the east, came asking to see the infant King of the Jews, whose Star they had seen in the sky. Herod was perturbed, as well he might be; as he was the king of the Jews. His advisors told him that the Messiah, the awaited deliverer of the Jews would be born in Bethlehem.

The Magi set out for Bethlehem, and saw the Star halt over the house where the Baby was. They offered gifts of gold, frankincense and myrrh. Joseph was warned in a dream to escape to Egypt. Herod, furious because the Magi did not return to him as he had requested, tried to get rid of a potential rival by killing all the young male children in the vicinity.

Luke's second chapter deals with the birth of Jesus. The Emperor Augustus decreed a census. Quirinius, governor of Syria, had to carry it out. Everyone had to move to his original family home, Joseph going from Nazareth to Bethlehem. Because the inn was crowded, Mary, suddenly in labour, had to lie her newborn infant in a manger. In the fields outside, shepherds had a vision of angels directing them to the birth of the Messiah in Bethlehem and singing in praise of God, and hurried off to find the Baby.

The first use of December 25 as Christmas Day dates from Rome in the year 336. To the pagan Romans, it was the birthday of the "Unconquered Sun." The emperor Constantine's family had worshipped the sun; his vision of the cross came to him from the sun. It was easy to transfer the festival to the Son of Righteousness. Under St. Peter's in Rome, Jesus was pictured driving the chariot of the sun through the sky.

Matthew tells of a star which guided the Magi. The Star of Bethlehem has attracted many theories. Some people have thought that Halley's Comet (visible in 12 BC) may have been the star; the astronomer Kepler proposed a conjunction of the planets Jupiter and Saturn in 7 BC.

Whatever the exact events, it is certain that Jesus was born of a human mother, Mary. Peasants and intellectuals, Jews and Gentiles, may have been the first celebrants of the birth of a different sort of king from Herod and a different sort authority from Rome.

Stars figured prominently in the lives of the ancients. The astrologers developed a pseudoscience, combined with religious beliefs, which dealt with the assumed influence of the stars on human affairs and with the foretelling of events on earth by their position in the heavens. To this day, stars are used as symbols.

Stars are in evidence in our churches and homes – the five-pointed stars during the Advent-Christmas-Epiphany season. The significance we attach to them comes from the Bible. In the Old Testament, the coming of the Savior is referred to under the figure of a star. Instead of cursing the children of Israel, Balsam blessed them in this prophecy: "A Star shall come forth out of Jacob, and a Scepter shall rise out of Israel." (Num 24:17)

The festival of Epiphany marks the Christmas for the Gentiles. In the New Testament account of the coming of the Wise Men to worship Christ, a star plays a prominent part, for it was seen by them in the East and it led them from Jerusalem to Bethlehem.

Stars (the real ones on the sky and the representations we make of them) are meaningful to Christians. They remind us of the Creator and His marvelous works. The psalmist calls the moon and the stars the handiwork of God's fingers. Even more, the star of his festival season points to the salvation performed by our blessed Savior, who through St. John tells us, "I am the Root and the Offspring of David, the bright Morning Star." (Rev 22; 16) May that Star always shine in our hearts!

Block Construction

This block looks difficult, but if you build up the pieces as indicated below, you should have no problem piecing it. Using the templates as needed, cut pieces based on your desired color scheme. Note that number 4 and 4a pieces are mirror images of each other.

- Combine one number 4 piece with one number 4a piece to make each "A" section. Make four of these sections.

- Sew the "A" Sections into pairs and sew these together to make the center.

- Make four "B" sections with number 6 pieces and number 5 triangles.

- Set these into the center section as indicated.

- Make four "C" Sections with number 4 and 4a pieces and a number 2 triangles.

- Set these into the center section as indicated.

- Set two number 2 triangles into each "C" section and sew on a number 1 triangle.

- Finally, set in two number 5 triangles on each side.

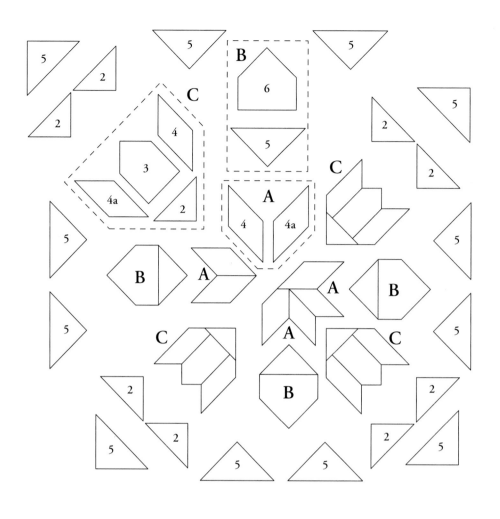

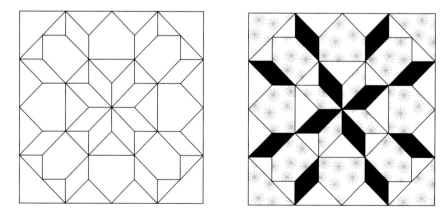

Finished Block

Templates

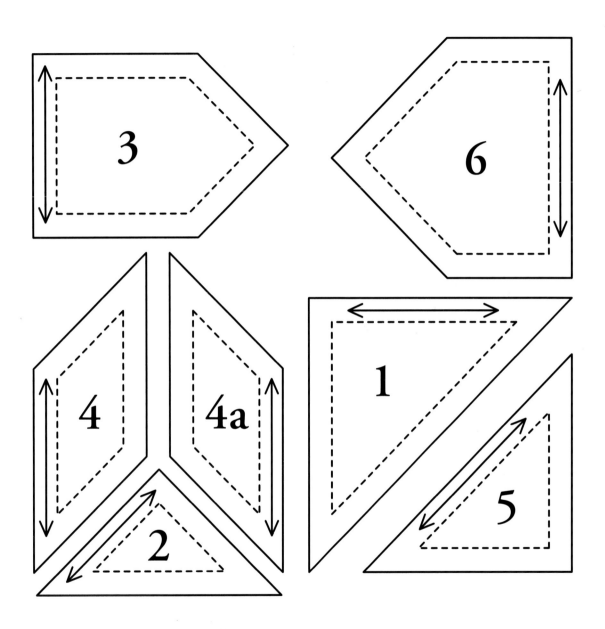

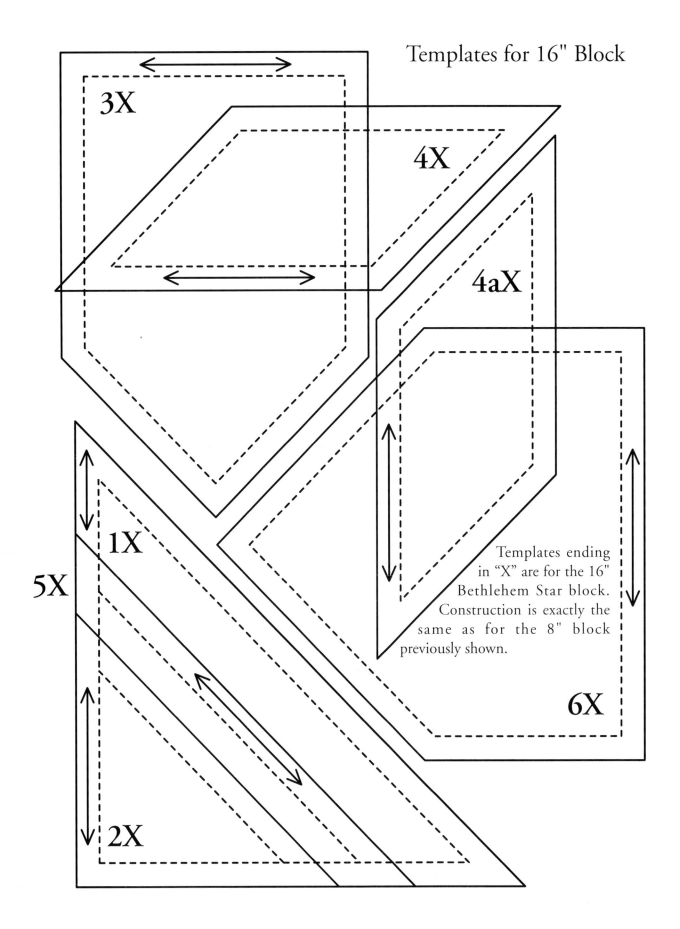

Templates for 16" Block

3X

4X

4aX

1X

5X

2X

Templates ending
in "X" are for the 16"
Bethlehem Star block.
Construction is exactly the
same as for the 8" block
previously shown.

6X

World Without End

"But Israel shall be saved in the Lord with an everlasting salvation: ye shall not be ashamed nor confounded world without end." (Isa 45:17)

America was founded on the principles of religious freedom, and many women made their church or religion the main focus of their lives. Thus, it would not be unusual to name this block, which forms an overall chain, World Without End. This name reflects their beliefs in Eternal Life.

World Without End is a name lifted from the Book of Common Prayer. Tory governors of the Crown very early brought to the land of Puritanism the ritual and ministers of the Episcopal Church. But the beautiful and striking language of the prayer book had never been forgotten, even by the most radical non-conformists. World Without End was, and still is, a phrase familiar in every church, no matter what creed.

"Glory be to the Father, and to the Son, and to the Holy Ghost; as it was in the beginning, is now and ever shall be, World Without End. Amen. Amen."

Block Construction

There are only three types of pieces to cut for this block. After you have determined your color scheme, cut the pieces (the example here is a two color block) and combine as shown.

- Make four "A" sections

  Attach a number 2 triangle to each side of the number 3 square.

  Set in a number 1 triangle into each side of the resulting piece.

- Sew these together in the proper pairs as dictated by the color scheme you have chosen.

A

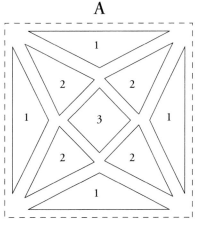

A

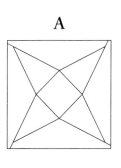

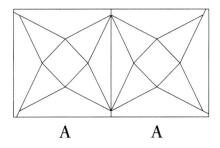

A   **A**

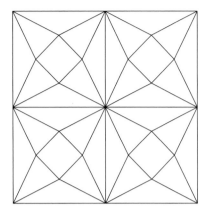 

Finished Block

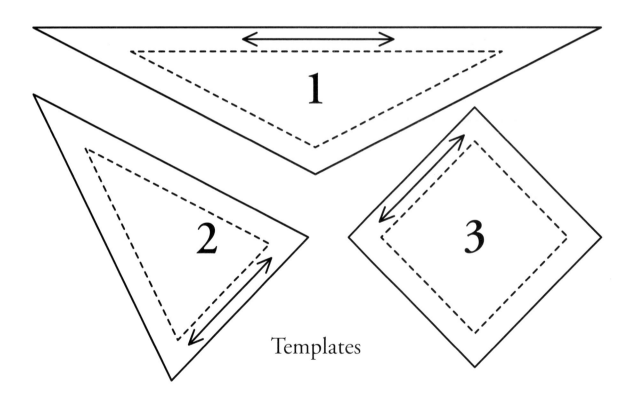

Templates

Lily of the Field

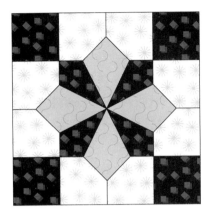

"Consider the lilies how they grow: they toil not, they spin not; and yet I say unto you, that Solomon in all his glory was not arrayed like one of them." (Luke 12:27)

"And why take ye thought for raiment? Consider the lilies of the field, how they grow; they toil not, neither do they spin." (Matt 6:28)

This is an unknown pattern gleaned from very old files. Twentieth century quilters have named it Lily of the Field. The most popular reference to the lily is in the above scriptures. These passages are not to be construed that one should not work for a living, but rather that one should not worry about earning a living, especially for the purpose of storing up wealth.

The Lily is also the symbol of purity and has become the flower of the Virgin. Originally, in Christian symbolism the lily was used as the attribute of the virgin saints. One incident in the life of the Virgin, the Annunciation, is particularly associated with lilies. Occasionally, the Infant Christ is represented offering a spray of lilies to a

saint. Here the lily symbolizes the virtue of chastity.

The Hebrew name shoshan or "whiteness" was used as the general name of several plants common to Syria, such as the tulip, iris, anemone, gladiolus, and ranunculus. Some interpret it with much probability, as denoting in the Old Testament the water lily or lotus. "It's flowers are large, and they are of a white color, with streaks of pink. They supplied models for other ornaments of the pillars and the molten sea." I Kings 7:19, 22, 26: "And the chapters that were upon the top of the pillars was lily work; so was the work of the pillars finished. And it was a hand breadth thick and the brim thereof was wrought like the brim of a cup, with flowers of lilies: it contained two thousand baths."

In the Canticles its beauty and fragrance shadow forth the preciousness of Christ to the Church. Groser, however, strongly argues that the work, both in the Old and New Testaments, denotes liliaceous plants in general, or if one genus is to be selected, that it must be the genus Iris, which is "large, vigorous, elegant in form, and gorgeous in colouring."

The lilies spoken of in the New Testament in Matthew 6:28 and Luke 12:27 were probably the scarlet martagon or "Red Turk's-cap lily, which naturally attract the attention of the hearers." (Balfour)

Of the true "floral glories of Palestine," the pheasant's eye, the ranunculus, and the anemone, the last named, is however, with the greatest probability regarded as the "lily of the field" to which our Lord refers. "Certainly," say Tristram, "if, in the wondrous richness of one plant can claim pre-eminence, it is the anemone, the most natural flower for our Lord to pluck and seize upon as an illustration, whether walking in the fields or sitting on the hillside."

These exotic-looking plants grow wild in the Middle East. A small flower, with large poppylike blossoms, anemones grow abundantly throughout Palestine.

The Greeks called the flower krihon, meaning "wind." Sometimes the plant is called "windflowers" and sometimes it is called "lily."

Scholars do not agree as to the exact translation of the Hebrew word Shoshan, which appears in the Scriptures as "lily of the valley" (Song of Sol 2:1-2), "among the lilies" (Song of Sol 2:16), and "lips like lilies." (Song of Sol 5:13)

A number of bulb flowers have been suggested for this lily: crocus, Easter lily, anemone, narcissus, iris, and tulip. The primary clue as to what the particular flower meant seems to lie in the content of each passage.

With their brilliant colors and unlimited shades, it is not difficult to imagine Jesus speaking of the anemone when He compared King Solomon to the "lilies of the field" in Matthew 6:28-29.

Block Construction

There are four separate shapes in this block. Once you have selected your color scheme, use the templates as necessary and cut the required pieces.

- Sew each number 3 triangle piece to a number 4 triangle piece.

- Sew two of these pairs together to form each half of the center of the block. Then sew these halves together to get the center.

- Sew two number 2 pieces together (in mirror image) to make two "B" sections and two "C" section centers.

- Add number 1 squares to either side of these last two to finish the "C" sections.

- Sew the "B" sections to either side of the center, then add the "C" sections to the top and bottom.

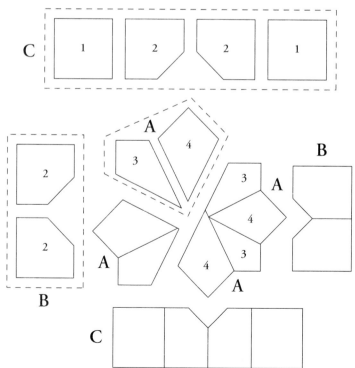

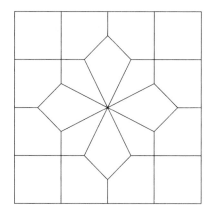 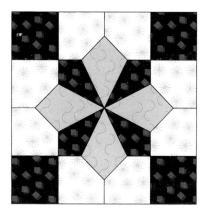

Finished Block

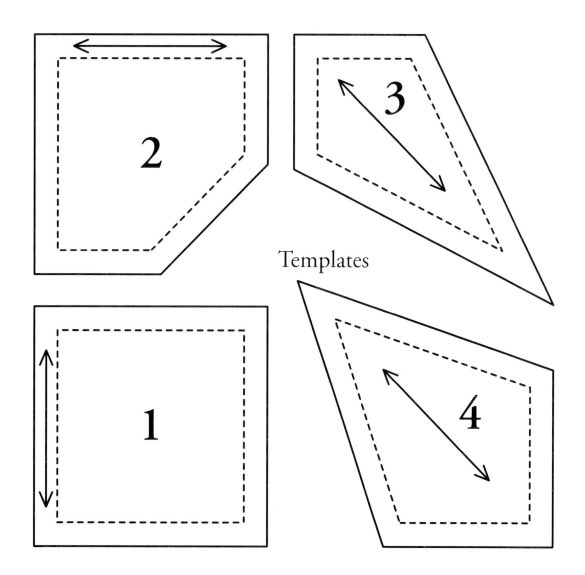

Templates

Storm At Sea

"**B**ut as they sailed, he fell asleep and there came down a storm of wind on the lake; and they were filled with water, and were in jeopardy. And they came to Him and awoke Him saying, 'Master, Master, we perish.' Then he arose and rebuked the wind and the raging of the water; and they ceased, and there was a calm." (Luke 8:23-24)

This pattern creates an optical illusion. While all lines are straight, you get a wave-like movement from all the angle changes.

And there arose a great storm of wind, and the waves beat into the ship, so that it was now full. And He was in the hinder part of ship asleep on a pillow: and they awake Him, and say unto Him, 'Master, carest thou not that we perish?' And He arose, and rebuked the wind, and said unto the sea, "Peace, be still." And the wind ceased, and there was a great calm. And He said unto them, "Why are ye so fearful? How is it that ye have no faith? And they feared exceedingly, and said one to another, 'What manner of Man is this, that even the wind and the sea obey Him?" (Mark 4:37-41)

Water is the symbol of cleansing and purifying. In this sense, it is used in the sacrament of baptism, symbolizing the washing away of sins and the rising to newness of life. It also denotes innocence as when Pilate publicly washed his hands, saying, "I am innocent of the blood of this Just person." (Matt 27:24) Often water suggests trouble or tribulation as in this block. "Save me, O God, for the waters are come into my soul. I am come into deep waters, where the floods overflow me." (Ps 69:1-2)

Block Construction

This block includes nine types of pieces. Once you choose your color scheme, simply use the templates as necessary, and cut the pieces indicated.

• For the "A" sections sew four number 2 triangles to the sides of each number 3 square. Sew the number 1 triangles to the sides of the resulting square.

• Sew two number 4 and two number 4a triangles to the sides of each number 5 diamond. These are the "B" sections.

• Sew a "B" section to both sides of two of the "A" sections. These are the top and bottom rows of the block.

• Sew the number 7 triangles to the number 8 square and add on the number 6 triangles to the sides of the resulting square to get the center section.

- Sew a "B" section to both sides of the center section to get the center row.

- Add the top and bottom rows to the center row.

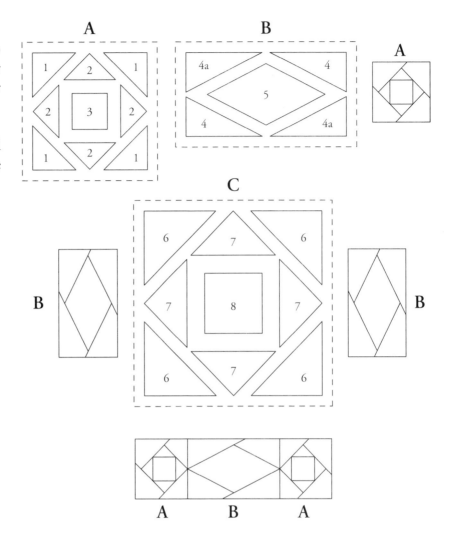

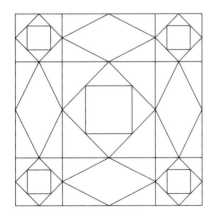
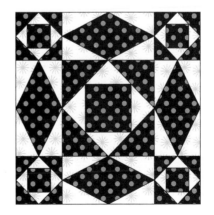

Finished Block

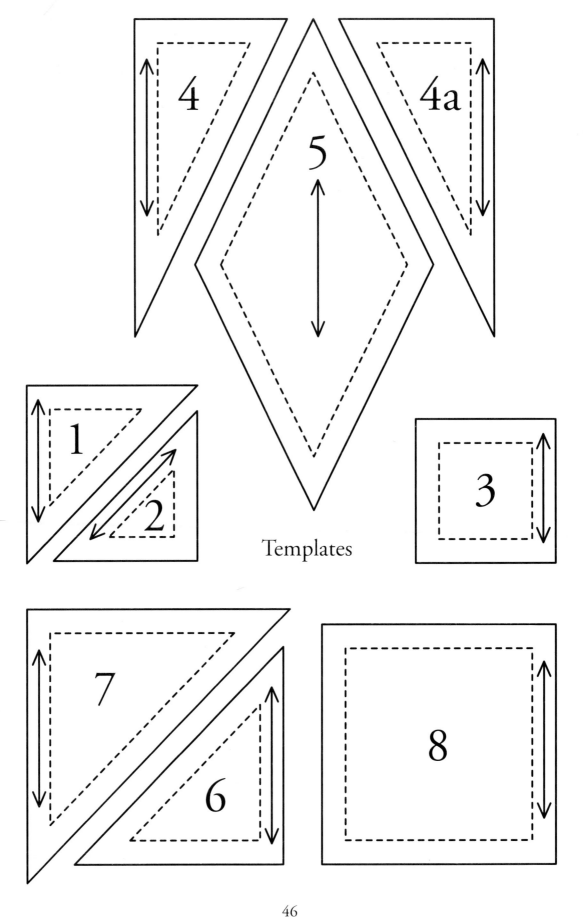

Templates

Job's Tears

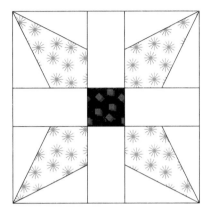

J ob (persecuted): "My friends scorn me but mine eyes poureth out tears unto God." (Job 16-20)

A great diversity of opinion exists as to the authorship of this book. From internal evidence such as the similarity of sentiment and language to those in Psalms and Proverbs, the prevalence of the idea of "wisdom" and the style and character of the composition – it is supposed by some to have been written in the time of David and Solomon. Others argue that it was written by Job himself or perhaps more probably by Moses, who was "learned in all the wisdom of the Egyptians, and mighty in words and deeds." (Acts 7:22) But the authorship is altogether uncertain.

The book of Job is a historical poem – one of the greatest and sublimest poems in all literature. Job was a historical grand person, and the localities and names are real. It is one of the grandest portions of the inspired Scriptures, a heavenly-replenished storehouse of comfort and instruction, the patriarchal Bible, and a precious monument of primitive theology. It is a didactic narrative in a dramatic form.

This book was apparently well-known in the days of Ezekiel, B.C. 600 (Ezek 14:14). It formed a part of the sacred Scriptures used by our Lord and His apostles, and is referred to as a part of the inspired Word. (I Cor 3:19)

The subject of the book is the trial of Job – its occasion, nature, endurance, and issue. It exhibits the harmony of the truths of revelation and the dealings of Providence, which are seen to be at once inscrutable, just, and merciful. It shows the blessedness of the truly pious, even amid sore afflictions, and thus ministers comfort and hope to tried believers of every age. It is a book of manifold instruction, and is profitable for doctrine, for reproof, for correction, and for instruction in righteousness. (2 Tim 3:16)

Job had raised his family, made his place in his village and was described as "perfect and upright." Job regularly prayed that his children be free from sin.

Job suddenly loses everything: his family, his flocks, and all he possessed. "Then Job rose, and rent his mantle, and shaved his head and fell down upon the ground, and worshipped, and said, 'Naked came I out of my Mother's womb, and naked shall I return thither: the Lord gave, and the Lord hath taken away; blessed be the name of the Lord.' In all this Job sinned not, nor charged God foolishly." (Job 1:20-22)

Satan again plots against Job and gives him a terrible disease, causing him great pain. Then begins a long and tortured poetic struggle of Job and Eliphaz, Zophar, and Bildad, his three friends, to perceive a God who is understanding.

The story concludes with a dramatic confrontation, when God speaks to Job out of a whirlwind. It is a caring God who answers Job and gives him recognition and respect. This firsthand experience is enough. Job puts his trust in God's power and wisdom, and accepts the Will of God in his life.

This story of reward and punishment, hope and despair, leaves us feeling somewhat uncomfortable in its lesson. It exposes man's greatest fear, that the God of Love we trust might intentionally bring misfortune to test our loyalty and faith. But thoughtful reasoning ultimately brings us to the realization that faith is a gift we must pray for and that we cannot judge all events from our perspective of limited understanding.

Perhaps the four points extending into the corners of this block represent the breadth of Job's material possessions and wealth, fragmented by the four intersecting lines representing a cross or, perhaps God.

"After this lived Job a hundred and forty years, and saw his sons, and his sons' sons, even four generations. So Job died, being old and full of days." (Job 42:16-17)

Block Construction

This is perhaps the simplest of these blocks to make, once you have selected fabrics and cut the pieces. There are five shapes.

- Sew a number 1 and number 1a triangle to opposites sides of each number 2 piece. These are the "A" sections.

- Sew an "A" section to both sides (one turned ¼ turn) of two number 4 rectangles. The result will be the top and bottom rows of the block.

- Sew the other number 4 rectangles endwise to the number 3 square. This will make the center row of the block.

- Sew the rows together.

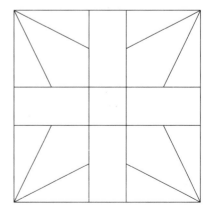

48

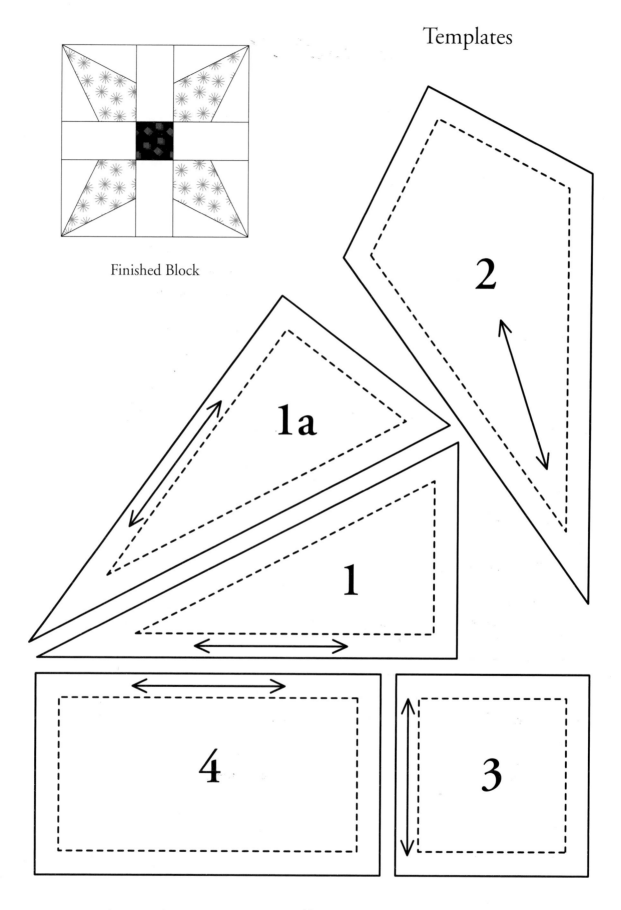

Finished Block

Templates

2

1a

1

4

3

Hosanna

"And the multitudes that went before, and that followed, cried, saying, 'Hosanna to the Son of David; blessed is He that cometh in the name of the Lord; Hosanna in the highest.'" (Matt 21:9)

The date palm is characteristic of Palestine. It is described as "flourishing" (Psalm 92:12), "upright". (Jer 10:5) "Rising with slender stems 40 or 50, at times even as much as 100 feet, its only branches, the feathery snow-like, pale green fronds from 6-12 feet long, bending from its top, the palm attracts the eye wherever it is seen." It is usually ten years before a date palm begins to bear fruit, and then it will bear every year from six to ten trusses of fruit, each containing hundreds of dates. In the olden days, Jericho was rightly named "The city of palm trees." (Deut 34.3) Palms were also to be found in the oasis of Engedi on the western shore of the Dead Sea. Engedi was also called Hazezontamar (Gen 14:7), which means the place of the cutting of the palms.

The tree is the symbol of the righteous.j57

(Ps 92:12) At the institution of the Feast of Tabernacles (Lev 23:40), palm leaves were prescribed as part of the foliage to be carried by those appearing joyfully before the presence of the Lord, and apparently the palm leaf was a very important part since the bunch of green branches, the lulabh in Hebrew, was named after it. Palm branches were symbolic of victory (Rev 7:9), and when Christ made his entry into Jerusalem, the crowds took branches of palm and went forth to meet Him. (John 12:13) This meaning of victory was carried into Christian symbolism, where the palm branch was used to suggest the martyr's triumph over death. Martyrs are often depicted with the palm either in place of, or in addition to the instruments of their martyrdom. Christ is often shown bearing the palm branch as a symbol of His triumph over sin and death.

A palm tree staff is the attribute of St. Christopher, in reference to the legend that he uprooted a palm tree to support himself on his travels. After carrying Christ across the river, he thrust the staff into the ground, whereupon it took root and bore fruit. A dress made of palm leaves is an attribute of St. Paul the hermit.

The branches of palm trees symbolize Jesus' triumphant entry into Jerusalem. We read in Matthew's gospel (21:8): "Most of the crowd spread their garments on the road, and others cut branches from the trees and spread them on the ground." The branches were plucked from palm trees in gardens and along the way, and they were plaited or twisted into a kind of matting green

Christ followers have a share in His triumph over sin, death, and the dead. Catechumens, who on Palm Sunday renew and confirm their baptismal vow with the Triune God, do so, not in reliance on their own strength, but on Christ's victory. While every catechumen has an individual confirmation verse, here is one common to all:

"Whatever is born of God overcomes the world; and this is the victory that overcomes the world, our faith. Who is it that overcomes the world but he who believes that Jesus is the Son of God?" (I John 5:4-5)

Today we carry palms in memory of our own confirmation.

In Christian symbolism, ashes are the symbol of penitence. On Ash Wednesday, the first day of Lent, ashes placed on the forehead express the penitential nature of the season. The ashes represent the death of the human body and symbolize the shortness of earthly life.

In 1823, the hymn, "Ride on, Ride on in Majesty!" was written specifically for Palm Sunday by Henry Hart Milman: "Ride on! Ride on in Majesty! Hark! all the tribes hosanna cry: Thy humble beast pursues his road with palms scatter'd, garments strowed. Ride on! Ride on in majesty! In lowly pomp ride on to die; O Christ, Thy triumph begin o'er captive death and conquer'd sin."

Milman's praise was poetic. Perhaps an early American woman was inspired to transfer her praise into the fabric art of her quilt top. The pattern of palm leaves known as Hosanna was pre-Revolutionary in origin; it was considered difficult to piece, with its long angular triangles and sharp points. The original inspiration for this quilt pattern is believed to have come from the Biblical account of Jesus' welcome into Jerusalem. Few patterns can rival Hosanna for its graphic and realistic representation, and it is a most fitting tribute to welcome Christ into one's heart and home.

Block Construction

There are 13 distinct shapes in this block. However, the construction is very simple. After choosing your fabrics, use the templates as necessary to cut the pieces and construct the block as shown.

- Sew each number 2 piece to a number 3 piece; number 4 piece to a number 5 piece; and number 6 piece to a number 7 piece. Be careful of the orientation of the pieces. Note the illustration.

- Sew each number 2a piece to a number 3a piece; number 4a piece to a number 5a piece; and number 6a piece to a number 7a piece. Be careful of the orientation of the pieces. Note the illustration.

- Sew the resulting 2-3 piece, 4-5 piece, and 6-7 pieces together in that order.

- Sew the resulting 2a-3a piece, 4a-5a piece, and 6a-7a pieces together in that order.

- Sew these two resulting pieces together to form a square with one corner missing.

- Set in the number 1 square into this space to get section "A".

- Sew four of these together to form the block. Note that these can go together in several different ways. The basic "A" section is the root of this block, resembling palm fronds, and can be combined in various ways as indicated on the next page.

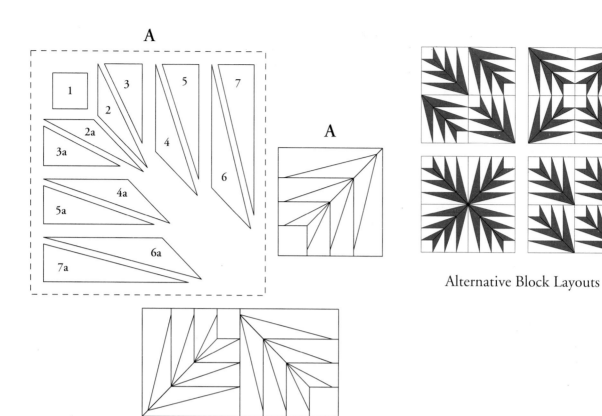

A

A

Alternative Block Layouts

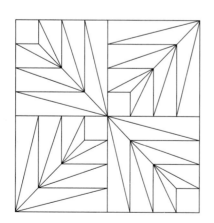

A   A

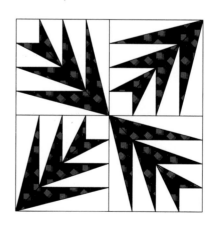

Finished Block

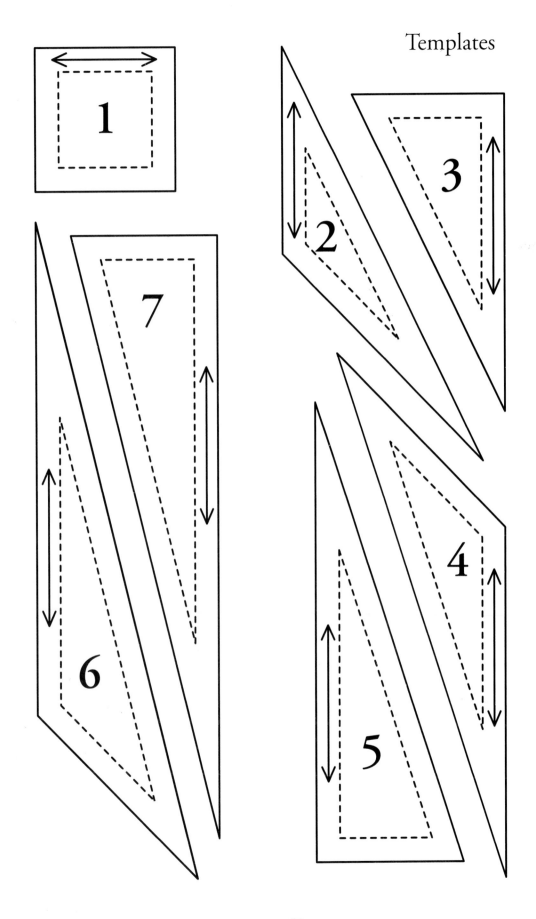

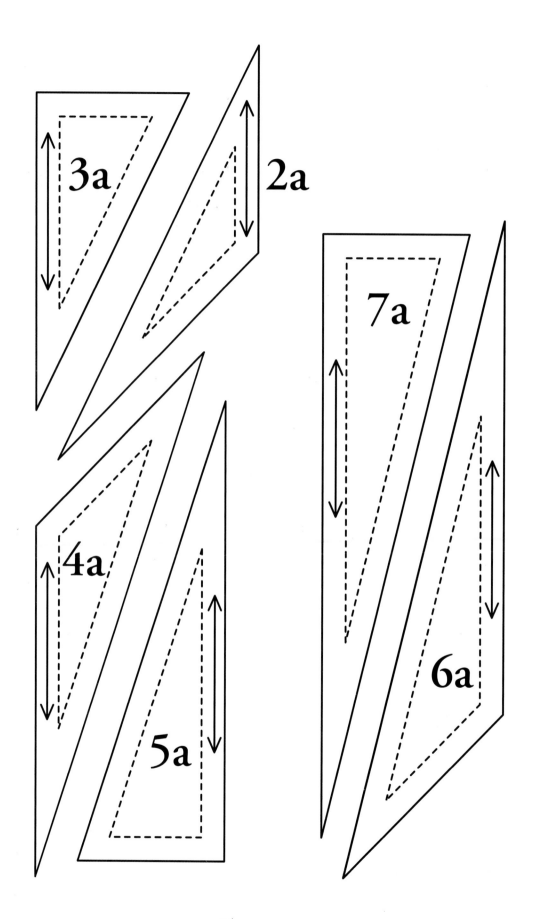

54

Quilting Designs
for
Alternate Blocks

The iris is a rival of the lily as the flower of the Virgin. It appears as a religious symbol in the works of early Flemish masters where it accompanies and replaces the lily in pictures with the Virgin. This symbolism stems from the fact that the name "iris" means "sword lily", which was taken as an illusion to the sorrow of the Virgin at the Passion of Christ.

Iris

"I will be as the dew unto Israel: He shall grow as the lily and cast forth his roots as Lebanon. His branches shall spread, and his beauty shall be as the olive tree, and his smell as Lebanon." (Hosea 14:5, 6)

"And he shall judge among many people, and rebuke strong nations afar off, and they shall beat their swords into plowshares, and their spears into pruning tools: Nations shall not lift up a sword against nation, neither shall they learn war anymore. But they shall sit every man under his vine and under his fig tree; and none shall make them afraid: for the mouth of the Lord of hosts hath spoken it." (Micha 4:3, 4)

Fig

The fig tree is occasionally used in place of the apple tree as the Tree of Knowledge in the Garden of Eden. The fig leaf appears in the story of the Fall of mankind in Genesis 3:7, "And the eyes of them both were opened, and they knew that they were naked; and they sewed fig leaves together and made themselves aprons." From this allusion to its leaf, the fig became a symbol of lust. Because of the many seeds it also has become a symbol for fertility. The fig trees shed their leaves in late fall. With the buds appearing in January and beginning to swell in the early spring. (Song of Sol 2:13) In late spring the leaves begin to appear heralding the approach of summer. (Matt 24:32) When the tree is in full foliage there is early fruit which is eaten unripe (Isa 28:4), and on the withered fig tree (Matt 21:19), the tree was lacking. By May, when the summer figs are visible, the early ones have usually fallen (Nahum 3:12 and in Rev 6:13), "The stars of heaven fell unto the earth, even as a fig tree casteth her untimely figs."

Myrrh was a component of the holy anointing oil (sweet cinnamon, sweet calamus, and olive oil (Exod 30:23), because of its delicate scent ("my fingers dripped with sweet smelling myrrh", Song of Sol 5:5). In Psalms 45:8 it was used as a perfume for scenting clothes, in Proverbs 7:17 for beds, as a beauty preparation in Ester 2:12, carried in chains in Isaiah 3:19, or worn on the breast in Song of Solomon 1:13. In Matthew 2:11, the gifts of the wise men consisted of gold, frankincense and myrrh. In John 19:39, Nicodemus presented a mixture of myrrh and aloes for Jesus' burial. In Mark 15:23, Myrrh was mixed with the wine at the Cross. It was customary for the Jews to give those condemned to death, wine mingled with myrrh. This was refused by Jesus in Mark 15:23.

Myrrh

"And they sat down to eat bread; and they lifted up their eyes and looked, and behold, a company of Ishmaelites came from Gilead with their camels bearing spicery and balm and myrrh, going to carry it down to Egypt." (Gen 37:25)

"For the Lord thy God will bring thee into a good land, of brooks and of waters and of fountains: In the plains of which the hills deep rivers break out a land of wheat, barley, and vineyards, wherein fig trees and pomegranates, and olive yards grow: a land of oil and honey." (Deut 8:7, 8)

Pomegranate

"Grained Apple" (Pomum Granatum) According to Scripture the pomegranate was common in Egypt (Num 20:5) and Palestine (23:23) (Deut. 8:8). The Romans called it Punicum Malum, meaning Carthaginian apple because they received it from Carthage. In Joel 1:12, the pomegranate tree is mentioned in the judgments of God.

The pomegranate produces an abundance of good things and therefore is symbolic of the fertile power of God's Word and the riches of His divine grace as stated in Isaiah 55:11 and Romans 5:20. Whenever the Bible names principal fruits or trees, the pomegranate is among them. (Deut 8:8; Hag 2:19; Joel 1:12) In I Samuel 14:2, it was said that Saul tarried under a pomegranate tree, he was there because it was a sacred tree and not for the shade produced by the tree. When spring rains are over, the tree would be in full foliage. In Song of Solomon 6:11, during the spring, the bridegroom went into the garden of nuts to see whether the pomegranates were budding.

The pomegranate is a fruit about the size of an orange, full of kernels contained in a delicious red pulp and its juice is as sweet as wine. The pomegranate was a favorite fruit mentioned in the bible many times and was even used as a pillar decoration in Solomon's temple. Grenade, a french word derived from the Latin malum granatum – an apple full of seed, bears a strong contrast as the first kills with its fragments, and the second gives life with its nourishment. The bursting pomegranate symbolizes that as Christ burst forth from the grave on Easter morning, so too will Christians burst their bonds of death. With its ring opened the pomegranate is a symbol of Christ's resurrection as an event and also of the blessings He imparts. The Good News of Christ's resurrection certainly assures all Christians of forgiveness, hope of a greater life to come, peace with God and of their own resurrection on the Last Day. In the beginning of his letter to the Ephesians, St. Paul says that God "has blessed us in Christ with every spiritual blessing." The pomegranate in Christian symbolism most often alludes to the Church because of the inner unity of countless seeds in one and the same fruit.

"And the Lord said unto Moses, take unto thee sweet spices, stacte, and onycha, and galbanum; these sweet spices with pure frankincense: of each shall there be a like weight. And thou shalt make it a perfume, a confection after the art of the apothecary, tempered together, pure and holy." (Exod 30;34, 35)

Frankincense

Frankincense is an odorous resin imported from Arabia (Jer 6:20), and also continues to grow in Palestine. It was an ingredient in the perfume of the sanctuary. (Exod 30:34), and was used as an accompaniment with meat (Lev 2:1, 16; 6:15; 24:7)). When burnt it emitted a fragrant odor and hence the incense became a symbol of the Divine name and an emblem of Prayer. (Ps 141:2; Luke 1:10; Rev 5; 8; 8:3)

The almond is a symbol of divine approval or favor based upon Numbers 17:1-8, in which it is told that Aaron was chosen to be the priest of the Lord through the miracle of his budding rod; and, behold, the rod of Aaron for the house of Levi was budded, and brought forth buds, and bloomed blossoms, and yielded almonds. It is with reference to this passage that the almonds became a symbol of the Virgin Mary. In Ecclesiastes 12:5, it is referred to as illustrative, probably, of the haste with which old age comes. Others still believe in the old interpretation that the almond tree bears its blossoms in the middle of winter on naked leafless stems, and at the time they are ready to fall they appear as white snowflakes. Thus the almond blossom is a fitting symbol of old age with its silvery hair and its wintry unfruitful condition. In Jeremiah 1:11, "I see a rod of an almond tree... for I will hasten my word to perform it". Because it appears that the almond tree never sleeps, it is a fitting symbol of vision.

Almond

"Also when they shall be afraid of that which is high, and fears shall be in the way, and the almond tree shall flourish, and the grasshopper shall be a burden, and desire shall fail: because man goeth too his long home, and the mourners go about the streets." (Eccl 12:5)

Peace
63" x 74"
Marti Louk, Carmel, IN

Alice's Refuge
65" x 77"
Alice Cunningham, Carmel, IN

Precious Memories
56" x 72"
Kaye England, Indianapolis, IN

Inspiration
65" x 77"
Ursula Zimmerman, Noblesville, IN
Quilted by Cecelia Purciful

My Garden of Eden
52" x 66"
Excelda W. Shaw, W. Lafayette, IN

A Celebration of Life
72" x72"
Brenda Papadakis, Indianapolis, IN

Incade Ye Mphilo
52" x 68"
Sandy Heminger, Akron, OH

Joseph's Confetti Coat
36" x 36"
Kaye England, Indianapolis, IN

A Closer Walk
36" x 36"
Brenda Papadakis, Indianapolis, IN
Quilted by Cec. Purciful

Evening Stars for Joseph
37" x 37"
Kaye England, Indianapolis, IN

Purple Majesty
37" x 37"
Kaye England, Indianapolis, IN
Quilted by Alice Cunningham

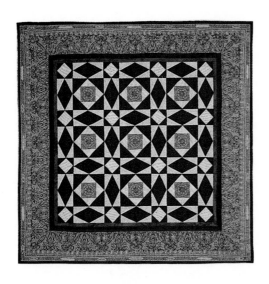

Genesis
30" x 30"
Joanie Rohn, Danville, IN

Star of Friendship
37" x 37"
Gachia Hoefer, Carmel, IN

Butterflies Are Free
36" x 36"
Kaye England, Indianapolis, IN

Inspiration
36" x 36"
Caryl Schuetz, Indianapolis, IN

Fruit of the Spirit
65" x 77"
Virginia Beck
Carmel, IN

Entwined in Vines
60" x 72"
Connie Clark, Sheridan, IN

Glory in Bethlehem
65" x 77"
Debra Danko
Greenfield, IN
Quilted by
Cecelia Purciful

*On the Road from
Jerusalem to Jericho*
52" x 64"
Lucille Garrett
Crawfordsville, IN
Quilted by Cecelia Purciful

On Eagles Wings
52" x 52"
Teresa Gunn
Indianapolis, IN

Back of quilt.

In the Garden
36" x 36"
Kaye England
Indianapolis, IN
Quilted by Cecelia Purciful

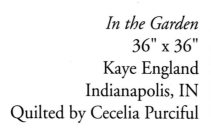

76

In the Beginning
36" x 36"
Kaye England
Indianapolis, IN

The Beauty of the Creation
42" x 42"
Kathleen Springer
Westfield, IN

Searching for Life
36" x 76"
Paula Guffy
Carmel, IN

Arbor Day
36" x 36"
Danita Rafalovich
Los Angeles, CA

Serenity
42" x 57"
Geneva Carroll
Carmel, IN

Favorite Things
65" x 77"
Janet Scott
Noblesville, IN

In the Vine
72" x 86"
Excelda Shaw
Lafayette, IN

Samsong
50" x 50"
Kathleen Saunders
Westfield, IN

Jacob's Journey
48" x 48"
Kaye England
Indianapolis, IN
Quilted by
Harriet Hargrave

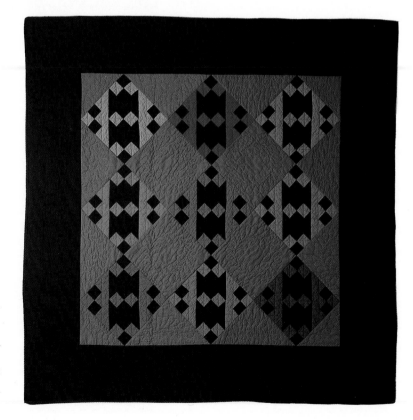

Comments from the Quilt Makers

Peace. I knew from the start the quilt would be for my son, Greg. What I didn't know was that the quilt would be for me too! What great therapy to work on this quilt after my mother died. I worked my way through all kinds of thoughts and feelings and had some great conversations with God, and by the time the binding went on, I felt I had regained some of the peace that had been missing in my life. *Marti Louk.*

Alice's Refuge. It is difficult to express in words what my "Bible Quilt" means to me – I have certainly been inspired. The first class literally brought tears to my eyes – bringing the same feelings I had as a small child hearing the truly wondrous stories of the Bible. The name of my quilt is taken from Psalm 46:1, "For God is our refuge and strength, a very present help in trouble." Quilting can be a haven during times of stress in our lives. *Alice Cunningham.*

Precious Memories. The name was chosen from a hymn by J. B. F. Wright of the same name. "As I travel on life's pathway, know what the years may hold." So true, but we are ever eager to make the journey. "As I ponder, hope grows fonder, Precious Memories flood my soul." I take great comfort in these lines and as I stitched the vines and leaves in the border I was reminded that hope abounds for all who believe and I was pleasantly consumed by all my thoughts. I chose strong bright colors to represent my belief that we all can be stars in this life and hereafter. Also, I believe Daddy and Rex will like this quilt. *Kaye England.*

Inspiration. I chose to use quilting stencils as appliqué designs to incorporate the plants from the Holy land in the border. I have been strip piecing for a few years and have made several quilts and wallhangings but when Kaye England and Quilt Quarters offered a class in Bible quilts, I was certain it was a perfect gift for my daughter-in-law. *Ursula Zimmerman.*

My Garden of Eden. The color green is used in this quilt because green symbolizes the plants in the Garden of Eden. I chose yellow for the alternate blocks because yellow reminds me of the sun in the garden and the Son who gives us light. It also provided the perfect background for quilting the plants of the Bible which I wanted in my garden. In the center of my garden I place the tree of life just as God did in Eden. *Excelda Shaw.*

A Celebration of Life. I did not know at the time I began this quilt that it would serve a dual role in my life, that of healing and of spiritual renewal. It is a celebration of life in honor of my father, who died recently. While working on the blocks I would find myself singing the old hymns of my youth and meditating about the Scriptures, renewing my faith.

The border was the most fun, as I love to appliqué. The pieces in the border and their meaning to me include: Cherub, presence of God; Harp, music; Rose of Sharon, romantic love; Cherry, good deeds; Pansy, remembrance; Peony, healing; Butterfly, resurrection; Dogwood, durability; Holly, crown of thorns; Pineapple, hospitality; Figs, fertility; Eagle, courage and inspiration; Iris, faith, hope, wisdom, and the Holy Trinity; Five-pointed Star, guiding star of the nativity; Heart, charity; Key, St. Peter; Fish, early Christians, Pear, Christ's love for man; Dove, Holy Spirit; Olive, peace; Olive branch, safe travel. *Brenda Papadakis.*

81

Incade Ye Mphilo. I decided to use African fabrics in this quilt because it would be a challenge I had not yet addressed in my quiltmaking. While making the quilt I attended a lecture on Afro-American quiltmaking in America, by Joyce Stafford and Ann Young. Joyce had an African exchange student (Reinette Mulangaphuma) living with her and I was able to share my quilt with Joyce and Reinette. Reinette told me that before Christianity came to the Zulu tribe their "bible" was the Incade Ye Mphilo, which translates into English as the Book of Life. We talked about the colors in the quilt and how colors have significance in the Zulu culture, that certain colors signify privileges within the group. Darker colors are worn by older members and brighter colors are reserved for childhood and symbolize a carefree spirit.

The *Tree of Life* block seemed to carry with it the most significance in this quilt. It was the last block I made and I tried to use an example of all the fabrics so that the leaves on the tree were symbolic of the "life" in the other eleven blocks, given to them by the color of the fabrics. In keeping with the theme of this project, *Incade Ye Mphilo* seemed to be the perfect name for this quilt. *Sandy Heminger.*

Joseph's Confetti Coat. This new fabric line was a perfect inspiration for this wallhanging. It was a natural for Joseph"s coat of many colors. We can only imagine the beauty of this great garment of love made for Joseph by his aged father. *Kaye England.*

A Closer Walk. This little quilt was made during the long process of making *A Celebration of Life*. I wanted to make a small, quick quilt in solids so I chose red and white: red for the Blood of the Lamb,

and white for the Virgin/Purity. The outer red border was appliquéd to resemble the curves in a crown. *Brenda Papadakis.*

Evening Star of Joseph. Another color variation of this great block using the stars as background. I imagined this brightly colored coat against an evening sky full of color and I was happy. *Kaye England.*

Purple Majesty. Job's Tears is a favorite block of mine so I elected to use it in this piece. I chose the colors green, symbolizing triumph of life over death, and purple, for its less used meaning of sorrow and penitence. Job was certainly triumphant in his later years but spent much of his life in sorrow. I felt the addition of the butterflies were a sign of rebirth for Job and his continued trust in God even though he suffered many trials. *Kaye England.*

Genesis. I have always been drawn to the Storm-at-Sea quilt, possibly seeing a correlation between the constant motion in the quilt and the seemingly constant chaos in my life. As I face my 40th birthday, I have decided to "Calm the Seas" and so have added the mariner's compass to guide me in beginning this new and exciting journey. *Joanie Rohn.*

Butterflies are Free. The Star of Bethlehem is symbolic of the birth of Jesus and a world forever changed by that event. I used the gray because it symbolizes the death of the body and the immortality of the spirit and the butterflies again represent His triumphant return. *Kaye England.*

Star Of Friendship. To me, this star means guidance. My friends guided me in making this quilt and made it a fun experience. What a gift from God my quilting friends are. *Gachia Hoefer.*

Inspiration. I made this quilt to look like an 1890's piece, having chosen fabrics and colors similar to those used in quilts of that time – dark blues, browns and tans, plaids and stripes. I have been studying and collecting quilts from the 1800's for years and as a result have made a few quilt projects which incorporate the style of this period. In designing this project, I also chose the old look because many bible pattern quilts were made during the 1800's. The butterflies were selected as much for their symbolism as beauty. To me, my quilt is inspirational, a symbol of my hope and faith. *Caryl Schuetz.*

Fruit of the Spirit. My main fabric was chosen as the black for the scene of the cross, the grapes for plants, and the gold for riches and Kings. My sashing represents earth, sky and water. *Virginia Beck.*

Entwined In Vines. Ecclesiastes 3-1 "To everything there is a season, and a time to every purpose". This quilt is dedicated to the memory of Cecil Bennett, a lovely lady who lived 96 years and told charming stories of growing up in a German Catholic home. *Connie Clark.*

Glory in Bethlehem. This is the first full size quilt I have completed and it reflects my interests. I enjoyed sharing the blocks with my fiends and family as I progressed. *Debra Danko.*

On the Road from Jerusalem to Jericho. I really liked the Christian symbols and the meanings of the colors. My favorite colors in this quilt are green and purple denoting New Life, royalty and power. I have numerous unfinished tops and this is the first quilt I have completed. I shall cherish this quilt forever. It has introduced me to a new aspect in quilting. *Lucille Garrett.*

On Eagles Wings. The name comes from a line in one of my favorite hymns based on Psalm 91. Whenever I sing that hymn, a special feeling comes over me and I am reminded of God's protection. I started my quilt during Lent and the colors I choose reflect this season of rebirth. I believe the only way to improve my quilting or anything in my life is to "stretch my wings and soar". *Teresa Gunn.*

In the Garden. A favorite old hymn came to mind as I finished this wallhanging. The Indiana Rose and Rose of Sharon certainly would bring to mind a beautiful garden. Growth of the spirit is as the flowers, in constant need of care if to flourish, and also a reminder that we do not come to the garden alone. *Kaye England.*

In the Beginning. Nothing is more representative of the beginning to me as the Tree of Life. It signifies the beginning of all mankind full of faults and full of hope. I see the tree as a symbol of family life. The use of green symbolizes the triumph of spring over winter, or life over death. I dedicate this project to my mother in hopes that she will find new hope and be triumphant in her recovery. *Kaye England.*

The Beauty of the Creation. The print used in the border was my inspiration for my quilt. I wanted to do something that reflected the natural beauty of the earth so I chose solid chintz to complement the elegance of the print. The three blocks used were Tree of Life, Storm at Sea and World Without End. *Kathleen Springer.*

Searching for Life. I felt that the four blocks that I chose for my quilt were telling me that searching is what life is all about. It is searching for heaven, for growth, for a better life, and for eternal life. The vine going around the quilt symbolizes God who surrounds us and who is always there when we need Him and is waiting for us to accept Him. The butterflies are a sign of the resurrection that tell us with our faith in God we can have eternal life. *Paula Guffey.*

Arbor Day. The Tree of Life block was an easy choice for me because of my botanical education. The Crown of Thorns wreath as the center block was chosen strictly for the graphics. Southern California has a subtle change of seasons and those gentle changes are represented in the four different tree color combinations, thus reminding me of Arbor Day. *Danita Rafalovich.*

Serenity. The Serenity Prayer has not only seen me through some tough times, but has taught me a lot. I am thankful for the simple, but powerful words in this prayer. The two flower bouquets I quilted into this quilt are reminiscent of my mother, grandmother and great grandmother's love affair with flowers. My version of God, placed in the top left corner, is watching over all.

Even though I am an intense person, I try not to take life too seriously – thus my use of the teal dachshunds on the back. Many of the fabrics used on the back were gifts from Kaye that she bought on her travels, so the back is an ode to Kaye! The Lily from the Lily of the Field block was used as a label to cover a flaw in the fabric and it didn't seem to fit anywhere on the front! While I was putting the label on the back, I watched as my hometown, Los Angeles, was burning itself down. I imagine that God was as sad as I was. I believe all creatures are equal in God's eyes, even teal dachshunds. In the midst of a hectic life, working on this quilt brought me a sense of peace and tranquility. *Geneva Carroll.*

Favorite Things. My first finished quilt and my first attempt at appliqué! As I worked on this quilt I was often reminded of the line from the Sound of Music song, "these are a few of my favorite things". From receiving the class as a gift to the last stitch in the binding I felt I was gathering my favorite things into one keepsake. *Janet Scott.*

In the Vine. The colors I chose for this quilt – reds, blues, purples, and lavender – symbolize love and truth, royalty and power. I wanted a stained glass effect because I love the stained glass windows of churches. The vine in the border symbolizes our new relationship to God from the cross (bottom) to the lamb (top) who sits upon the throne. The dove is a symbol of our baptism. *Excelda Shaw.*

Samsong. I started this quilt because I felt left out of the fun everyone was having making projects in the Bible quilt class. It is dedicated to my bird, Sam who used to sit on my sewing machine chirping away while I sewed. He was sick for several weeks while I worked on this quilt and died the day after I completed the quilt top. I quilted golden birds around the *Tree of Life* block in his memory. *Kathleen Saunders.*

Jacobs Journey. A collection of hand-dyed solids combined with black and cocoa brown were the start of this project. Jacob certainly had a long journey and the different color of blocks used represented stages of his life. Black, his sickness; green for regeneration of the soul through good works; purple, a sign of earned power; red for emotions; gold for divinity; and brown to symbolize the years Jacob spent in service or the barren years of his life. *Kaye England.*

Appliqué Designs

The designs on the following pages are for appliqué. Trace these designs to use as templates for making the appliqué pieces. Place these in the borders or alternate blocks of your quilt. Directions for needle-turn appliqué and my method for appliquéing vines can be found in the *Construction, Advice, Hints, and Tips* section of this book.

Amaryllis and Dove Appliqués

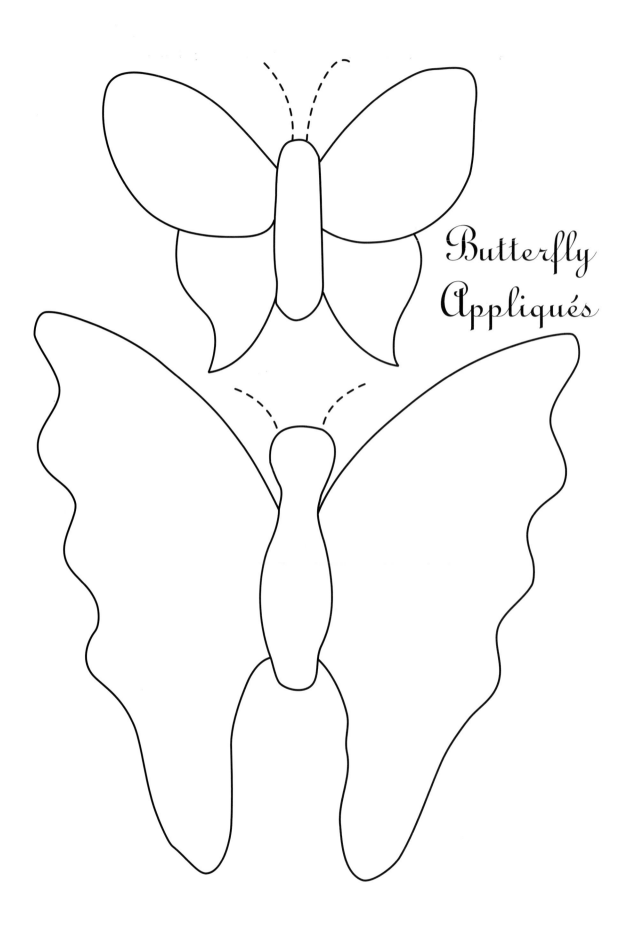

Butterfly
Appliqués

Indiana Rose Appliqué

Pomegranate Appliqué

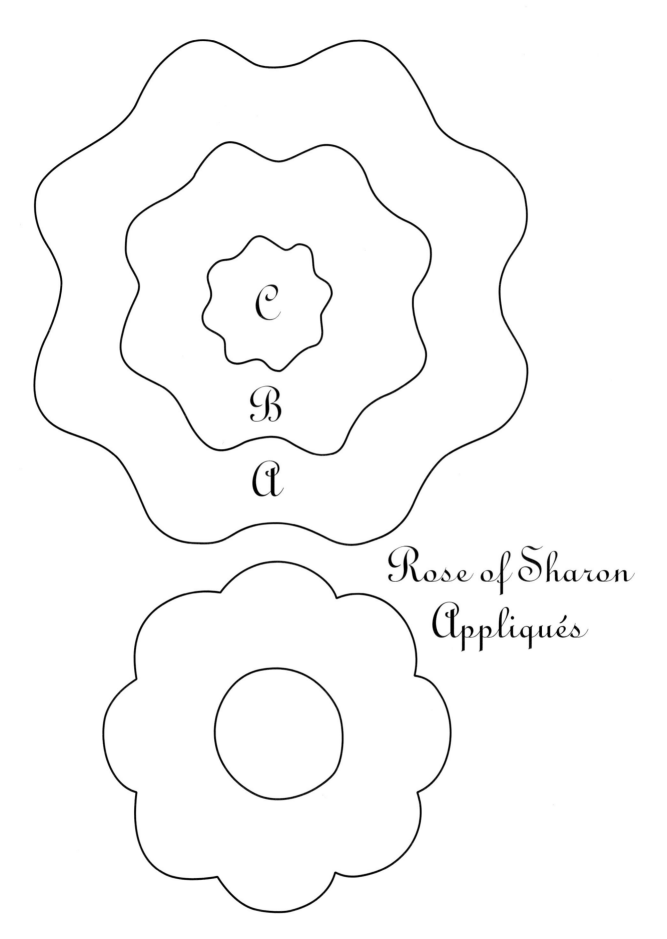

C

B

A

Rose of Sharon
Appliqués

Rose of Sharon Variation
Appliqués

Leaf Appliqués

Quilt Layout Options

Design and Layout Considerations

When you make this quilt, you will be considering many things in the design, not the least of which are what blocks to use and the layout of the blocks. You saw on the photograph pages that there are many ways to color the blocks to get a desired effect. You probably noticed also that there is a wide variety of layouts. Many of the quilts are complete 12 block layouts (with alternate plain blocks for quilting.) The placement of the blocks within the quilt can be done in a multitude of ways, depending on your preferences. This section emphasizes the options available in standard layouts with fewer blocks, variations, and single block layouts with 16" blocks (templates are provided for Joseph's Coat, Bethlehem Star, and Tree of Life.) Please refer to the referenced photographs.

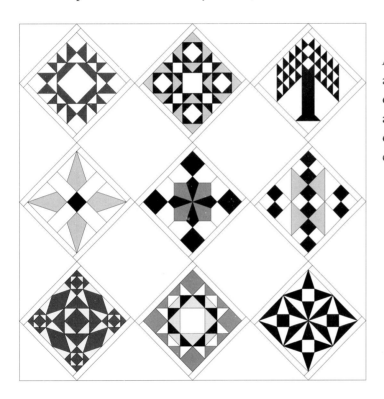

A simple nine block layout is a natural option for a square quilt. Here a variety of blocks are used. See Teresa Gunn's quilt on page 76 for an example.

Here is an example of a five block design with straight blocks and no sashing. This design requires an odd number of rows, with an odd number of blocks in each row. See Brenda Papadakis' quilt on page 72.

95

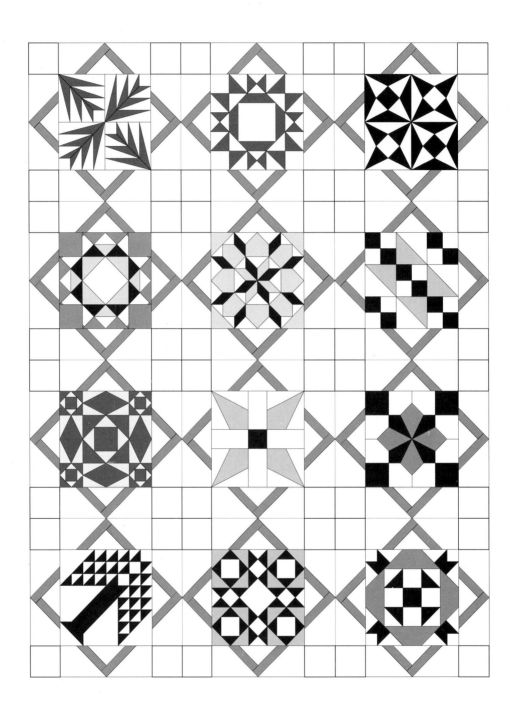

Most of the designs here set the blocks in a diagonal set. This design from Sandy Heminger sets the blocks straight, but still in a diagonal set. See Sandy Heminger's quilt on page 71.

Here is a five block approach, replacing the center quilting block with a pieced block. See page 76.

Here is another five block approach using one primary block (e.g., Tree of Life) and replacing the quilting block with another pieced block. Notice that the side triangles are pieced. There are seemingly infinite possibilities. See Danita Rafalovich's quilt on page 79.

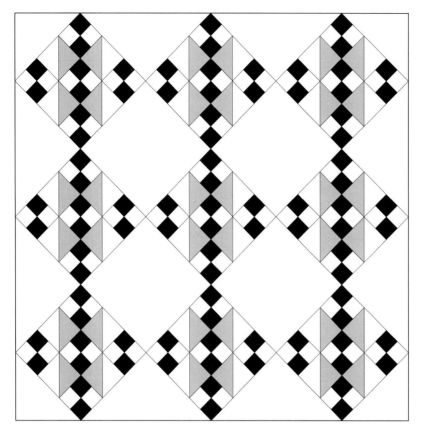

Here is a different approach, using the nine block layout, but using no sashing around the blocks. In addition, here I used a single block repeated. Simple. See page 80.

Another approach to block usage, as illustrated here, is using appliqué instead of quilting. This opens up endless possibilities in your design. See page 72.

You can combine the 16" blocks and the 8" blocks in many ways. Here is an example of the 16" Tree of Life block on point in conjunction with 8" blocks not on point. See Kathleen Saunders's quilt on page 80.

The 16" blocks make a great wallhanging. Here the Bethlehem Star is set on point. See the quilt on page 73.

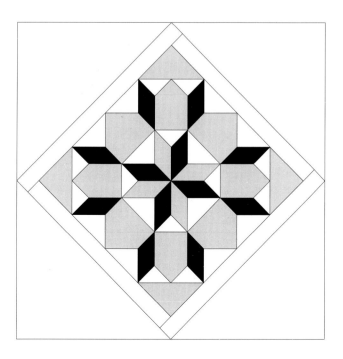

A simple subset of the main quilt is the four block column, proving a tapestry wallhanging. Again, a variety of approaches to block selection may be used. See Paula Guffy's quilt on page 77.

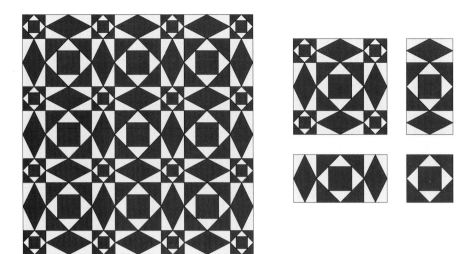

Some blocks lend themselves to tiling compositions, such as Storm at Sea, shown here. This one is pieced with the main block sashed with portions of the block. See Joanie Rohn's quilt on page 73.

Another subsection of the main quilt is the six block variation. This also may be made with a variety of block selection options. See Geneva Carroll's quilt on page 78.

Construction Advice, Hints, and Tips

Thoughts from Kaye

After much study and trial, I found that one of the best color pulls for this quilt was to select a main fabric, preferably with a close design, a background (don't feel bound to use beige), and three or four accent prints. Most importantly, be sure you have some variety in scale and form. After looking at the finished quilts in the book you will see there certainly are many ways to choose for this quilt, but I feel this will assure you of a great quilt. Don't be afraid to use more colors if the quilt needs some life. Study the color meanings and perhaps one of these will give you a color scheme for your quilt. The overall plan is for an alternate block with a different color, and again being used in the border.

Yardage Requirements

This generous yardage is for the complete quilt with the 8" finished blocks. I've found this gives you some options and will allow for some errors. If your quilt will be larger than 90", you will have to adjust for more yardage. I suggest auditioning colors before making choices for final blocks.

Background – 3½ yards
> This allows for a 9" border if appliqué is used. Cut down one side of fabric so border will not have to be pieced.

Alternate block – 3 yards
> This allows for a 3" outside border.

Main block fabric – 2 yards

Accent fabrics – ⅓ yard each

Backing – 5 yards

Color Symbolism

Color symbolism plays a very big role in the Bible and I hope that the following list helps you in some way when you begin.

Black is a symbol of death and also suggests mourning and sickness.

Blue symbolizes Heaven and heavenly love, It can also symbolize the color of truth, because the sky always appears blue after a storm, suggesting the unveiling of truth.

Brown symbolizes spiritual death and degradation and renunciation of the world.

Gray is the color of ashes (Lenten season) and signifies mourning and humility.

Green is the color of spring and new vegetation, symbolizing the triumph of sprint over winter.

Purple is associated with royalty and the sign of imperial power and is often used as a symbol of God the Father. It can also be the color of sorrow and penitence.

Red, the color of blood, is associated with the emotions and is symbolic of both love and hate.

Violet also symbolizes love as well as truth, passion, and suffering.

White is accepted as the symbol of innocence, purity, and holiness. It is often used for the Virgin.

Yellow has a twofold meaning. Golden yellow symbolizes the sun and divinity. On the other hand yellow also suggests infernal light, jealousy, treason, and deceit.

Hand or Machine Piecing

Your first decision will be to piece this by hand or machine. Most of the blocks will piece very well on the machine. If you are experienced, everything can be done this way. The directions here are for hand piecing. I think the choice of how to piece depends entirely on your life at the time. Hand piecing is certainly relaxing and is very mobile. I haven't seen a sewing machine on the little league field or in the doctors office, but I have seen hand piecers there. You make the choice. Certainly the rules are a little different.

Make sure you have all your supplies on hand, including needles, fine pins, scissors and thread to match your fabric. I prefer to use 100% cotton thread with 100% cotton fabric. Never cut your thread longer than 18", as it tends to knot-up and tangle.

Determine the sequence of assembly ahead of time an lay out your design. I prefer to work on a fleece board (foam core covered with fleece) to lay out and also to stand back and view my color choices.

Pressing

To steam or not to steam, that is the question. I say steam if you want weird shaped pieces, otherwise don't steam. Steam is like a vice we have – used in moderation it's okay, but overused it is deadly. Most people iron as if they were really mad at the fabric and therefore can completely change the shape without realizing it. A dry iron has less chance to distort your piecing, especially if working with bias edges. Remember to let the iron glide by itself and not to ride on it. In our classes, we teach how to make rainbows out of triangles. It's

real easy with steam. If you prefer working with steam, by all means do so. Just be careful and be aware of the dangers. When pressing appliqué, I prefer to press face down in a towel and then I use steam, but not to excess.

Templates

I prefer to trace the pattern onto a piece of template material, using a fine line pen or pencil. Quarter inch seam allowances are provided in all of the templates in this book.

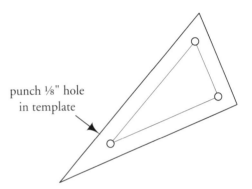

punch ⅛" hole in template

Punch a hole in the template (with ⅛" hole puncher, available at most stationery stores) at seam intersections. Place the template on

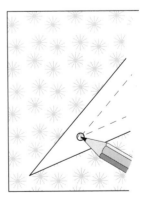

the wrong side of the fabric, being aware of grainline, and trace around the template. Mark seam intersections and draw lines between the marks. Align seam intersections

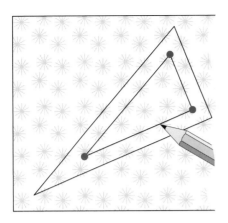

using the marks, and sew on lines between marks. Be sure to use good scissors (or rotary cutter if you wish) to cut your fabric.

Piecing

Choose the two pieces you are joining and put right sides together. Pin at each corner where pencil lines meet and once in the middle. Most right-handed people will generally sew right to left and lefties left to right. Your stitch will be the same. I start by taking a small back stitch and then start my running stitches. Continue across your line occasionally taking a backstitch to strengthen. At the end of the seam I again

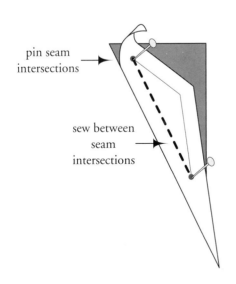

pin seam intersections

sew between seam intersections

take a backstitch to lock the stitch. Using a small needle (size 10-12 between) will give you more stitches to the inch.

Setting In

If you have to set a piece into a section (A), place the piece to be set in right sides together with the section (B). Line up

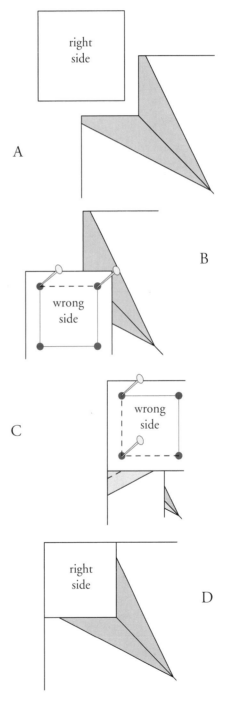

right side

A

wrong side

B

C

wrong side

D

right side

105

seams, pin and sew between seam intersections. Press open. Fold over unsewn seam, align seams, pin intersections, and sew (C). Press open (D).

Needle-turn Appliqué

There are so many great appliqué books on the market that I hope you find time to study them. I feel this is a tough topic to cover in just a few paragraphs. There are many ways to appliqué, but for this project I will discuss needle-turn only.

Unlike piecing, your appliqué shape is marked on the right side of the fabric with the sewing line visible, forcing you to turn under the seam allowances as you go. I prefer to use a #11 sharp needle for appliqué

and thread to match the piece. Bring the needle up and through the back of the fabric and through the fold of the top fabric, passing back down slightly ahead of the previous stitch. Small stitches no more

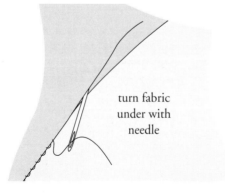

turn fabric under with needle

than ⅛" are desirable. With the tip of the needle, turn under as you move around the pattern piece.

Alternate Blocks and Construction

Many of the quilts in this book include sashing around the main blocks, depending on the design chosen by the quiltmaker. The sashing can be any width. Once sashing is applied, measure the unfinished main block, including sashing, and cut squares of this size from your background or alternate fabric.

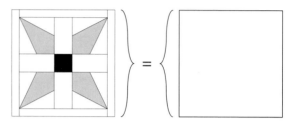

To construct the quilt in a diagonal set, sew the main blocks and alternate blocks together in diagonal rows, capping the ends with outside triangles or corner triangles as appropriate. Sew the row together.

Outside and Corner Triangles

For the outside triangles, cut squares with sides equal to the main block diagonal plus

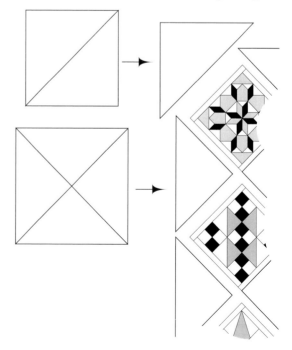

3". Cut these into quarters. For the corner triangles, cut squares equal to the block diagonal plus ½". Cut these on the diagonal. Attach these as appropriate to the ends of the diagonal rows of main blocks and alternate blocks.

Making the Vines

Cut the vine fabric on the bias 1½" wide. Study to determine how you wish your vine to flow. I recommend marking the final movement lightly with pencil until the final effect is achieved. Fold the vine in half, being careful on sharp curves not to stretch

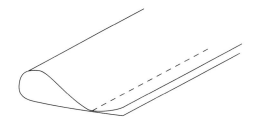

as you sew or your background will distort. If you are placing designs at the corners or in the center, it is not necessary to have a continuous vine, as you will be covering it at the intersecting points. After applying all vines on the machine, you may then fold over and appliqué by hand or machine.

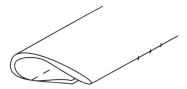

This method is very quick and almost foolproof. It doesn't matter if your seam allowance varies as vines are different widths and it gives your quilt a realistic look. After applying vines, your appliqué choices are limitless. Look for any type of design that means something to you.

Further study into Christian symbolism offers many choices. I have included a few designs, but as you can see from the photographs, each person has added her own touches. I would hope you stretch yourself to do the same. You may choose not to appliqué at all and that still produces a great quilt. Even if you have never appliquéd, I believe you will find this technique for your vines very easy.

For cutting leaves, I just free-hand mine. Any shape and size looks great on this type of quilt. If you are not comfortable doing this, refer to books or use the shapes we have given you. Most importantly, let the design be part of your planning and make it uniquely yours.

Making the Sandwich

To sandwich your quilt, lay prepared back out on flat surface. (For my back, I choose to sew strips on each side of the larger piece. this way I have two seams down the back, rather than one down the center.) Have a friend help you smooth the quilt back and then using masking tape, hold the back in position. Place batt on back and then add the quilt top. Make sure your back and batt are larger than the top.

Working from the center out, baste all three layers together. You may use large running stitches for this. Baste from the center to one side, then from the center to the opposite side. Then baste from the center to the top and from the center to the bottom. Then follow this technique for basting to the corners. If necessary, put basting stitches between these, always radiating out in one direction, then the opposite direction.

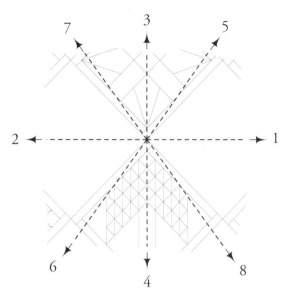

When basting from one side of the quilt to the opposite side, I start with a long thread, baste to one side, leaving enough thread at the center to rethread my needle and baste to the opposite side. An alternate approach is to always start at the center with a backstitch and baste outward.

Applying borders

There are two types of borders. Square borders can be applied by attaching pieces to two opposite sides of the quilt. To determine the length of these pieces, measure across the quilt at its center. Next

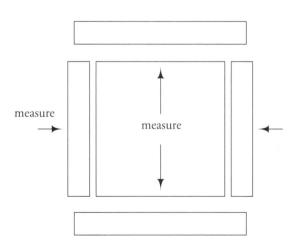

measure the other dimension of the quilt with these two sides attached, again at the center of the quilt. Cut border pieces of this length and attach them to the remaining sides of the quilt.

Mitered borders are more appropriate if you will be appliquéing in the border. Attach border strips to all sides, using a length equal to the quilt dimension plus two border widths plus seam allowances. Fold the quilt top right sides together over a 45° angle measured at the corner to be mitered. Sew at the 45° angle and trim.

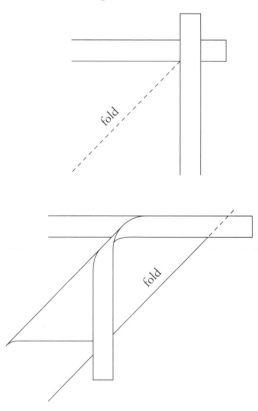

Applying the Binding

Cut strips of bias fabric 2½". Fold in half (don't press), and sew to the edge of the sandwiched quilt, aligning raw edges to the outside (¼" seam). Fold the binding over the seam to the back of the quilt and whip stitch into place. Cut bindings on the bias if

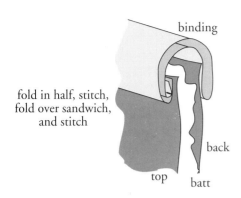

binding

fold in half, stitch,
fold over sandwich,
and stitch

back

top batt

it is necessary to do so (for example, to make a stripe go a certain way.) I don't usually cut on the bias.

To attach the binding in a corner, sew the binding on as indicated above, sewing to within ¼" of the corner. Turn the binding up, folding at a 45° angle. Then fold the binding down over the top of this fold so

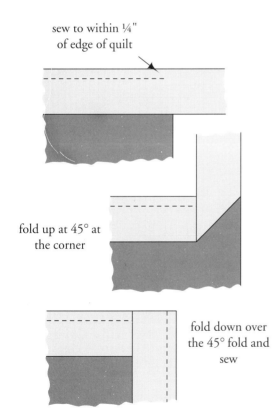

sew to within ¼"
of edge of quilt

fold up at 45° at
the corner

fold down over
the 45° fold and
sew

the edge of the binding is even with the top of the quilt and the side. Sew from the corner.

Quilting will finish your quilt by adding depth and dimension to the designs. Quilting is simply the same running stitch except through three layers instead of one. I really feel you should try to quilt with nothing smaller than a 10 between needle. If you use a large needle it becomes more difficult to achieve tiny even stitches. You should practice keeping your stitches even, top and bottom – I prefer larger, even stitches to small, uneven ones. As in most things, if you have a plan that works for you then stay with it. Again use a small length of thread to quilt, no longer than 18". When hand quilting I choose to avoid knotting the thread. I feel if you can pop the knot through to start, somewhere during the quilt life it will pop back out. Instead I float the needle and backstitch before quilting then backstitch and float when I end a thread.

To float the needle, start by inserting the length of needle through the top into the batt (not through the back!). Bring the needle out until only the eye is still inside

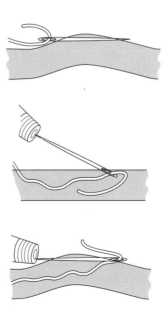

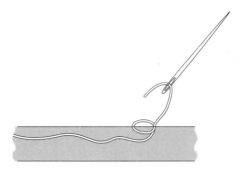

the quilt. Turn the needle point back away from the direction of quilting, and, with your thimble, push the eye end of the needle forward in the batt another length of the needle. Bring the needle back out, eye first, but not all the way. You will have floated the needle two needle lengths and may continue in this way, or, if starting a thread, you may backstitch and begin. I prefer to have approximately 3" of thread floating at the start and end of a quilting thread. This will leave the tail in between the layers and you can hardly pull this out. Before I backstitch at the beginning of a

thread I pull the loose end into the quilt. After backstitching and floating the needle at the end of a thread, I pull it taut and cut it, forcing the thread to pull back into the quilt.

Quilt Care and Fabric Care

We could discuss this subject for months and months and still not agree on the final results. I do not wash my fabric before use, but I do test for colorfastness. This is such an important topic, I prefer to tell you what I do and then have you make your own choices. I highly recommend the book, *Heirloom Machine Quilting*, by Harriet Hargrave. She has a textile background and thoroughly discusses this topic in her book. I think a lot of questions have gone unanswered until now on the care of textiles. As in all things, you must do what works for you, but I just can't make myself wash fabric that isn't dirty!

Bibliography

Brackman, Barbara, *Clues in the Calico*, Virginia: EPM Publications, 1989.

Brackman, Barbara, *Encyclopedia of Pieced Quilt Patterns*, Kansas: Prairie Flower Publishing, 1979.

Comay, Joan, *Who's Who in the Old Testament*, Weidenfeld & Nicholson, 1971,

Davis, J. D., *Dictionary of the Bible*, New Jersey: Fleming H. Revell, 1924.

Doty, William G., *Letters in Primitive Christianity*, Pennsylvania: Fortress Press, 1973.

Doubleday, *Great Events of Bible Times*, New York: Doubleday, 1987.

Dreyfus, Henry, *Symbol Sourcebook*, New York: McGraw Hill, 1972.

Dunton, William Rush Jr., *Old Quilts*, Maine: Self Published, 1946.

Ferguson, George, *Signs and Symbols in Christian Art*, New York: Oxford University Press, 1954.

Finley, Ruth E., *Old Patchwork Quilts*, Massachusetts: Charles T. Branford, 1929.

Fox, Sandi, *Wrapped in Glory*, New York: Thames & Hudson, 1990.

Fry, Gladys Marie, *Stitched From the Soul*, New York: Dutton Studio Books, 1990.

Gordon, C., *The World of the Old Testament*, New York: Doubleday, 1953.

Hopkins, Mary Ellen, *The It's Okay If You Sit On My Quilt Book*, Santa Monica, CA: ME Publications, 1989.

Irwin, John Rice, *A People and their Quilts*, W. Chester, PA: Schiffer Publications, 1984.

Judge, Edwin A., *The Social Patterns of Christians in the First Century*, Illinois: Tyndale House, 1960.

Khin, Yvonne M., *Collector's Dictionary of Quilt Names & Patterns*, Washington, D. C.: Acropolis, 1980.

Kinart, Malvina and Crisler, Janet, *Loaves & Fishes*, Connecticut: Keats Publishing, 1975.

Lansansky, Jeanette, *In the Heart of Pennsylvania*, Pennsylvania, Oral Traditions, 1985.

Bibliography, continued

Lehner, Ernest & Johanna, *Folklore & Symbolism of Flowers*, Plants, & Trees, Tudor Pub.

Liby, Shirley, *Bible Blocks, Old & New*, Indiana: Graphics Unlimited; 1991.

Martin, Nancy J., *Pieces of the Past*, Bothell, WA: That Patchwork Place, 1986.

Martin, Nancy J., *Threads of Time*, Bothell, WA: That Patchwork Place, 1990.

McClun, Diana and Nownes, Laura, *Quilts, Quilts, Quilts*, San Francisco, CA: Quilt Digest Press, 1988.

Orlofsky, Patsy & Myrol, *Quilts in America*, New York: McGraw Hill, 1974.

Payne, Suzy and Murwin, Susan, *Creative American Quilting*, New Jersey: Fleming H. Revell, 1983.

Pearlman, Moshe, *In the Footsteps of the Prophets*, New York: Thomas Crowell, 1975.

Potter, Charles Francis, *Is that in the Bible*, Connecticut: Fawcett Publishing, 1962.

Quilt World, *Bible Quilt Blocks*, Pennsylvania: House of White Birches, 1984.

Rehmel, Judy, *Patchwork Patterns from Bible Stories*, Minnesota: Åugsberg Fortress.

Sienkiewicz, Elly, *Spoken Without a Word*, Washington, D. C.: Turtle Press, 1983.

Squire, Helen, *A Quilters Garden*, New Jersey: Fleming H. Revell, 1987.

Untermeyer, Louis, *Plants of the Bible*, New York: Golden Press.

Wallis, Charles, *Holy Holy Land*, New York: Harper & Row, 1969.

Webster, Marie D., *Quilts, Their Stories and How to Make Them*, New York: Doubleday, 1915.

Zohary, Michael, *Plants of the Bible*, New York: Cambridge University.